Nothing Beats a Failure But a Try

Nothing Beats a Failure But a Try: A Memoir

by Phillip E. Jones

Path Press, Inc.
Original & Reprint Publishers
Evanston, Illinois

Library of Congress Cataloging -in- Publication Data
Designed by Phillip E. Jones and Aaron Foster

Names: Jones, Phillip E., 1940-author.
Title: Nothing beats a failure but a try / By Phillip E. Phillip E. Jones.
Description: Evanston, Illinois : Path Press. Inc., [2019] | Summary: "This
autobiography
relates the experiences of an African American educator beginning on the
Southside of Chicago until he became a professor and college administrator
primarily at the University of Iowa. The author relates his involvement with
faculty and students as well as programs which he established"-- Provided by
publisher.
Identifiers: LCCN 2019022454 | ISBN 9780910671187 (Paperback)
Subjects :LCSH: Jones, Phillip E./ 1940- | African American
educators--Illinois--Chicago--Biography. | African American
teachers--Illinois--Chicago--Biography. | African American
(Higher) --Illinois--Chicago--Biography.

Send inquiries to:
Path Press, Inc.
Post Office Box 5683
Evanston, Illinois 60204
pathpressinc@aol.com

TABLE OF CONTENTS

FOREWORD

When the invitation from Gerald Early to contribute to this issue of <u>Daedalus.</u> arrived in late February last year, I was commencing a ritual of mile-long walks and conversations with Phil Jones, an old friend and colleague at the University of Iowa. I had been trying to control the physical symptoms of diabetes, and Phil was kind enough to suggest that we walk for a mile or so every two days at a nearby mall. Phil had only recently been fired from his position as vice president for student services and dean of students at the University of Iowa. The public reason for his dismissal was that university officials were not satisfied with his handling of an incident involving several black student athletes and a white student. A white male official had also been fired for the very same alleged "neglect." Phil had served the University for forty years but was let go without a hearing. In return, Phil sued the University for what he believes was his unjust dismissal. Then he began to write a book about his experiences at Iowa beginning in the 1960s, when he first arrived as a student, and tracing his career there until the time of his dismissal as a vice president.

Phil asked me to read drafts of each section of the work-in-progress so that we could discuss them while we walked. His vivid recollections prompted me to recall my own encounters with institutional powers, not at Iowa but elsewhere. What struck me about Phil's writing was not his anger, which was not at all visible, but the affectionate relationships he had shared with his colleagues and peers. From university presidents to departmental chairmen to bureaucratic officials he encountered during his years at Iowa, he wrote nothing negative about anyone. Rather, he captured the nuances, the day-to-day actions of his well-meaning colleagues, who were deeply involved in creating a bureaucratic structure of affirmative-action – the Educational Opportunity Program (EOP) – intended to include, support, and nurture students from minority groups. Reading Phil's detailed recollections, I saw the portrait of a muscular bureaucratic structure that must have evolved within universities in all parts of the country during the 1960s, 1970s, and 1980s.

What was striking to me was Iowa's institutional receptivity to non-white students, especially black Americans. Phil described one major contributor to the University, a philanthropist named Roy Carver, who said to him in 1971, "I told you I was going to do something for the colored boys." The same Roy Carver also contributed to the building of the Carver-Hawkeye Arena and additions to the University Hospital. For many years I wondered what formed the basis of that receptivity and generosity but could only speculate on the effectiveness of laws promoting inclusion and "affirmative action." Now I truly believe that these developments at Iowa evolved out of a unique spiritual dimension of the State of Iowa's population. One senses this trait, which I have begun to call "neighboring," in Iowa store clerks, garbage collectors, postmen and women, young people, and, most especially, in senior citizens. When Phil and I walked through the mall, we are constantly greeted by passing strangers. If I had to capture this quality in language, I would employ the ancient Greek word pneuma, meaning "the vital spirit of life itself," whether at work or during times of worship, and especially during times of giving. Indeed, pneuma is foundational in all systems of religious belief, but it seems to me that, as a civic conviction, it is still vital as well in communities rooted in rural mores. Why else would construction workers feel more comfortable beginning their work at dawn? Why else would farmers' markets remain so popular among residents of urban area that are overstocked with discount supermarkets? And why else would communities like Iowa City, as well as its university, go to such lengths to attract, and then to maintain – long before the advent of "affirmative action" – so many black students, as well as those from other minority groups? And what, particularly now, is causing so many institutions to retreat from this noble stance? There are the tensions caused by the Tea Party and its increasing numbers in all areas of the country. There is the legislative focus on Latino immigrants and the rising call to exclude them from protections offered by the Fourteenth Amendment. Add to this list the declining popularity of Obama as the nation's first black American president.

During our long walks and conversations, I found myself repeating to Phil Jones a phrase I had absorbed many years ago from my conversations with Henry Nash Smith, a Mark Twain scholar and professor at the University of California, Berkeley. Touching on the political and aesthetic polarization of the 1960s and 1970s, Professor Smith employed, repeatedly, the term "bureaucratization of the pneuma," meaning that the spiritual dimensions and processes of American life were increasingly being subjected to bureaucratic control. In my interactions with Phil Jones, I tried to recall a time when bureaucratic power was not as visible in Iowa City as it is today.

James Alan McPherson, Emeritus Professor in the University of Iowa Writers Workshop, was the first Black writer to receive the Pulitzer Prize for Fiction in 1978. This excerpt reprinted from Daedalus winter 2011 essay "Pursuit of the Pneuma."

His many national awards include a Guggenheim Fellowship and the MacArthur "Genius" Fellowship.

Acknowledgments

When I was appointed to an entry level staff position in the admissions office at the University of Iowa in 1968, I had no idea I would ever write a memoir. I had the good fortune to be associated with staff colleagues who knew the value of archival materials. I am grateful to the foresight of Sheila Vedder, Cheryl Bates, and Belinda Marner for excellent staff assistance during my forty-year career.

I want to recognize the students because without them there are no stories to tell. I have thought about many of them in the process of recollection. Although I have cited only a few, they symbolize the many students – both minority and majority I taught, learned from, advised, disciplined, and assisted.

I thank the late Robert Engel, professor of education, and Horace Porter, professor and head of American Studies and African American Studies, for their invaluable critiques, guidance, and encouragement during the development of multiple early manuscript drafts. Thanks also goes to Joseph "Joe" Brisben for editorial comments in the final drafting process.

I am pleased and honored to recognize and acknowledge my niece, Meryn Fluker, and nephew, Brett Erskine Jones, former University of Iowa students, who assisted me with this project. A graduate in journalism, Meryn edited the entire manuscript. Brett attended Iowa two years before transferring to the University of Illinois, Chicago, where he earned his degree in graphic art. He created a cover design for the book.

I received constant counsel and encouragement from friend and colleague Penny Edgert and Yvonne S. Leftwich. I am indebted to my "type-A home girl" Betty Bolden – and her University of Illinois henchwomen – for their oversight of the project.

I especially want to recognize my friend the late James Alan McPherson. Our conversations during our frequent mall walks were enlightening to me in a unique way.

Finally, thank you Jo Lavera, Phyllis, and Joel for always caring for me and my many initiatives that interrupted your lives as we made this journey together.

Introduction

"If you want to be the boss, you gotta pay the cost. Learn baby, learn." I didn't value academic preparation nearly as much as I should have when I was growing up. Instead, I relied on lessons I learned through stories from older African Americans in our vernacular culture. I'm a walking testament to the efficacy of common sense sayings that express an emotion that may fit a problem or situation encountered in life. I take seriously folk sayings about life lessons that are applicable to contemporary experiences.

Segregation and discrimination are historic limitations of life chances for African Americans. Dr. Martin Luther King Jr. was a leader in the movement to advance educational and economic opportunities for Black people. King was assassinated on April 4, 1968. In his honor, University of Iowa President Howard Bowen created the Martin Luther King Jr. Scholarship Program to increase enrollment and educational opportunities for African American students – Educational Opportunity Programs (EOP).

Dean of Admissions and Records Donald Rhodes recruited me to begin the initiative. Other universities created similar programs. Black recruiters responded to Black students' demands for inclusion in the life of the university. Their cries didn't sound like the complaints university administrators typically heard from the largely white student bodies dominating their institutions. Instead, the legitimate laments from Black students shared a timbre I recognized: the vernacular culture in which I was well-versed.

Like a riff on a jazz theme, platitudes comprise a litany of responses to students' problems, as an improvisational expression of relevant experiences related to the emotion in the statement of the problem. In many situations, relating a relevant life situation a student can identify with is more meaningful than an abstract response that correctly identifies a problem, but doesn't help the student identify with the solution. As these students spoke, their words reminded me of different emotional experiences I'd had in my life. When recruiting, I frequently used folk sayings in the Black vernacular tradition to illustrate my point and inform the situation at hand. In doing so, I spoke a language few college administrators knew at that time.

Vernacular expressions generated cross-cultural communication across racial lines among students, faculty, and staff.

I envisioned my appointment as an opportunity to improve upon what I experienced as an undergraduate on the predominantly white campus of the University of Illinois in Urbana-Champaign at the beginning of the 1960s. Prior to the beginning of the EOP movement, retention programs were not a university priority. Little had been written about equity for disadvantaged students at predominantly white colleges and universities. Systematic methods to identify, finance, and provide academic support for Black students became evident in response to student demands during the late '60s and early '70s. Consequently, many institutional efforts were done in piecemeal fashion.

Initially, the emphasis was on developing compensatory programs. Their purpose was to minimize financial and academic impediments faced by minority/low-income students at traditional, competitive, predominantly white, selective schools. However, faculties and administrators found themselves operating in a new cultural context with few effective sources of prior experience to address the learning styles and cultural vernaculars of so-called "disadvantaged students." Universities recognized the need for social change – sometimes after campus disruptions.

University administrators across the country appointed EOP directors to create social change programs on campuses. In 1968, each university in the consortium of Big Ten universities and the University of Chicago (the Committee on Institutional Cooperation – CIC) appointed Black male and female administrators to initiate systematic recruitment of Black and other minority students. We were relatively young, with master's degrees, but we came from outside of higher education. Our major responsibility was to relate to Black students. We spoke the vernacular because our bosses couldn't.

Admissions standards were broadened – or lowered, depending on who's talking. Our charge was to find talented, bright, ambitious students. We stressed education and economic disadvantage, but all Black students weren't disadvantaged in the same way or to the same extent. To be sure, a disadvantaged student at a select private university wasn't necessarily disadvantaged at an open enrollment public university or community college.

As EOP directors, our job was to find the students, get them admitted with adequate financial aid, nurture, motivate, and help them endure frequent hostile encounters in predominantly white communities. Just as we related to these new college students, we also had to teach them the lexicon of their white peers. Along with my fellow new hires, I was expected to relate to and counsel the campus administration and faculty on the attitudes and behaviors of Black students –

even though our backgrounds were more similar to those of our students than compatible with the campus culture. We had to learn to serve both constituencies, by becoming acculturated to the campus politics and cultures we often encountered – and usually we were the only people of color in the administration. Few if any of us had secure faculty positions with little or no social-cultural support system for our own personal well-being.

The federal government played an important role in establishing equity programs in secondary schools and postsecondary institutions. Affirmative action resulted from expanding equity in educational opportunities.

Pain accompanied this progress. The backgrounds of minority individuals – both students and staff – taken from outside the traditional culture of the predominantly white academic tradition, infused a sense of concern for social change in the development for all students in the university. These perceptions of concern changed the college experience to be more sensitive to the rights of all students for freedom of expression, to add more relevance in the curriculum, become a more multicultural intellectual institution, and to enhance excellence and diversity in the learning experience. This historical narrative moves around in time to explain and show connections between lessons learned from historic events in society, higher education, and my experiences that were relevant to the development of the EOP concept and the creation of social change through organizational development.

When I began as an admissions coordinator (de facto Black recruiter), I was aware of the significance of my appointment in relation to the momentous assassination of the leading African American in the American Civil Rights Movement. I lived through – and was emotionally affected by – the sit-in demonstrations by southern Black college students as I watched the revolution unfold in media and the urban revolts of Black citizens across the nation.

In the years between 1968 and the start of the 21st century, it became abundantly clear to me that my appointment at Iowa had broader implications for social change than I realized when I started. My first appointment was a precedent for social change in higher education related to freedom of speech and expression, employment opportunities, and housing availability. Initially, Black students were the objective of recruitment, but that quickly morphed to include Native Americans, Latinos, Asians, women, the disabled, and people of various sexual orientations.

Indigenous expertise derives from the life experiences, common sense teachings, achievements and setbacks of life in African American culture – otherwise called the blues idiom. It all prepared me for my initial position at the University of Iowa and led to my career as a teacher, counselor, administrator, consultant, and advocate for the human rights of all.

Chapter One:

BRONZEVILLE

My generation began after the depression era of the 1930s and before the baby boomer generation after the Second World War in the mid-1940s. My parents' generation of Black Americans began the northern migration during the 1920s and 1930s.

My mother migrated to Gary, Indiana, where she had a sister and brother who had moved there years earlier. In Gary, my mother married and had a child. The marriage didn't work. While separated and in the process of divorcing my sister Frankie's father, Momma became pregnant with me. She wanted to keep her pregnancy a secret from her husband and his family out of fear of losing custody of her nearly year-old daughter after the divorce. Only my Aunt Jessie in Gary knew about Momma's pregnancy. I was born in Chicago, Illinois, in 1940.

I'm the result of my mother's choice to have a child as a single parent. While I grew up without a father, Momma took her responsibility seriously. I was taught at a very early age to recognize that I was responsible to her and only her for my behavior. She worked hard to provide for my sister and me, as well as for my two younger sisters. Momma taught us to take initiative and be responsible for our actions.

In the mid-1940s Momma learned of an opportunity to move out of our small basement apartment next to a coal bin and garbage cans on the South Side at 31ˢᵗ and Michigan Ave – across the street from the Illinois Institute of Technology – in a gray stone building which had been a multi-level one family residence. My Uncle Henry, who had originally gone to Gary to work in the steel mills, was pastor of a small African Methodist Episcopal (AME) Zion church in the converted living and dining rooms of the first floor of the building. A new public housing project was being constructed on West 37th Street and Wentworth on the fringe of the historically Irish and Polish Bridgeport community.

I remember Momma telling us about going to St. James Catholic Church on 29th Street and Wabash Avenue before dawn one morning in 1946 to get in line to apply for a two-bedroom apartment in the Wentworth Gardens Public Housing Projects. Public housing was designed for poor people. Veterans, the elderly and low-income families with children were given priority. Our family, consisting of a mother and two children supported by a federal welfare program called Aid to Dependent Children (ADC), qualified for the housing. Project apartments were nice compared to our previous apartment in the basement under Uncle Henry's small church.

Concrete building communities were designed with multiple play areas with swings, seesaws and a small playground. In the early years, residents were required to keep apartments in excellent condition. The housing authority would inspect each apartment annually. When various criteria were not met, such as an unkempt stove or refrigerator, tenants were assessed fines and families could be evicted for failure to pay rent or for chronic unacceptable behavior.

Bridgeport was a white ethnic, working class, predominantly Catholic community. Our neighborhood was a public housing project – named Wentworth Gardens – for Black working-class families. We lived in social and economic segregation, separated by the Pennsylvania Railroad viaduct.

I sold newspapers and scorecards at the ballpark – Comiskey Park (now U.S. Cellular Field), home of the Chicago White Sox three blocks north of the projects. I saw the white crowds enjoying amenities I knew we didn't have, but I didn't feel deprived. "You don't miss what you've never had," was a perspective reinforced in adult conversations I heard growing up. I believed we lived in a good neighborhood.

The 37th Street School, later renamed Robert S. Abbott after the African American founder of the Black oriented The Chicago Defender newspaper, sat a block away from my house.

Although I didn't always act accordingly in elementary school, Momma raised us to believe that, regardless of where we came from, we should endeavor to achieve excellence and make something of ourselves. My mother emphasized learning. Born in 1912, she was the youngest of ten children and the only one to complete formal primary education. She was sent to boarding school and later went to the all-Black Alabama State College in Montgomery where she completed a two-year teacher training program. She then taught in segregated rural schools in Alabama during the Great Depression.

Momma often read to my sister Frankie and me before we were old enough to start school. We started at the Douglas Elementary School. When I was in the second grade, Frankie and I transferred into the 37th Street School. It was overcrowded to the point that we went to school half-days and sat two to a desk with between 30 and 36 children in a classroom. The principal and almost all the teachers were white while all the students were Black. We had well-worn textbooks, shared one book at each desk and handed them in after each lesson. To relieve overcrowding, temporary mobile classrooms were brought in while construction began on a new building.

In second, third, and fourth grades I was not a good student. My older sister loved reading and learned to read before entering kindergarten. Me, I was having fun playing and not paying attention to our evening lessons at home or to teachers at school.

In fifth grade, we began to take standardized reading tests. I scored at the third-grade level on the first test. My sister, who was a year ahead of me in school, was reading at the eighth- or ninth-grade level. I was held back a grade while Frankie skipped ahead one grade level. When I was in sixth grade we were tested again: I only advanced one year, to reading at the fourth-grade level, while my sister was reading at the level of senior high school. Once again, I failed, and Frankie skipped ahead.

I had a discipline problem and was suspended from school for fighting in class. Teachers said they didn't like my attitude. I felt they didn't care about me as a person. Going into seventh grade, no teachers wanted me in their classrooms.

One teacher, however, agreed to save me from being sent to reform school. Her name was Mrs. Harriet D. Brown. She imposed strict discipline on her classes and especially on me. She and my mother agreed this was best for me. I was made to understand that Mrs. Brown spoke for my mother. She often didn't allow me to go out for recess – I had to read inside instead. I generally stayed in the classroom during lunch when my behavior dictated.

Under Mrs. Brown I and other children in class learned the discipline necessary for productive learning. She expected excellence, stressed doing your best, whatever the outcome, until we excelled as much as we were capable. She taught by precept and example. She often told us about what she was learning as she pursued and eventually earned a master's degree from Chicago's Roosevelt University. To demonstrate the rewards of learning, she took the class to her commencement ceremony. She showed us day-by-day how hard work and achievement go hand-in-hand. She knew her students and their families, and she often spoke up for us with other teachers. The principal and her colleagues respected her highly.

One of her techniques to get students to read critically was to have us outline chapters from a textbook. We learned how thoughts were organized, and we were required to summarize various sections in our own words. We were given time limits for completing the tasks, which encouraged us to improve reading speed and understanding. At the same time, Mrs. Brown gave me the responsibility of delivering packages to the Board of Education in downtown Chicago which bolstered my self-confidence and improved my image with other teachers and staff in the school.

When Mrs. Brown began working on a doctorate degree in education at the University of Chicago, she would often help me with reading by having me accompany her to Ida Noyes Hall on campus while she studied for her degree. For the first time, I could imagine myself going to college. Through both subtle and explicit ways, Mrs. Brown taught me and my classmates to have pride in ourselves and confidence in our abilities to learn regardless of how poorly we had previously performed.

In the eighth grade, I was being tested again and my reading score went up to the tenth-grade level. I went on to earn admission to Tilden Technical High School – a select high school emphasizing technical and college preparation. Throughout my time in high school and college I faced other struggles but, due to the lesson from my mother and reinforced by Mrs. Brown, I always believed that I would overcome my learning disadvantages if I put forth my best effort.

After I began working at the University of Iowa, I went to visit Mrs. Brown. She had intermittently worked on her doctorate for several years at the University of Chicago. I asked her to consider transferring to the University of Iowa as a full-time graduate student to complete her doctoral studies. In 1980, Mrs. Brown earned a PhD from the University of Iowa College of Education. The title of her dissertation is "A Study to Identify and Describe Characteristics of Avid Readers in an Inner-City Grade Five Classroom."

I recounted that story in 2004, at the University of Iowa's Belin-Blank International Center for Gifted Education and Talent Development, when I was invited to make a presentation at a symposium about a teacher who made a significant impact on my young life.

Lessons arrive quickly and unexpectedly in early life. These experiences contribute to the formation of basic values. I learned that any experience is a good experience if you learn from it. I didn't just learn from adults like Momma and Mrs. Brown.

When I was in fifth grade, before being placed in Mrs. Brown's classroom, I got into a fight with a boy who had bullied me since fourth grade. We were at the age when boys and girls begin to like each other. There was a girl in my row who seemed to like me. Away from the teacher's gaze, my bully would do little things to get the girl's attention. At first, I was unaffected by his actions, but at some point, he turned his attention to me. As I sat at my desk near the front of the classroom one morning,

I wasn't in a playful mood and didn't want to get in trouble with the teacher – even though I seemed to have had a habit of doing something that would get me into trouble with a classroom teacher and earn a trip to the office. That day, I didn't want to court trouble.

Suddenly, he balled up a piece of paper and threw it in my face. I felt fear and embarrassment. Suddenly, I lost my cool. I didn't care about the teacher or anyone else in the room. In blind rage, I jumped from my desk across the aisle and grabbed him by his face. I don't remember much else about what happened until the teacher separated us after we wrestled to the front of the room and behind a large upright piano sitting in the corner.

She took us to the assistant principal's office. I remember the boy beginning to make peace with me by devising a story about how we were playing around but not fighting. I hadn't noticed under one eye the bruise he had that I apparently caused. I wasn't sure how I did it, but I felt bad about hurting him. My sympathy for him erased my fear of him.

As she had many times before, my mother arrived at school to see the assistant principal. I was suspended for a week, both for fighting in class and for supposedly hitting the teacher while she was separating us. It was the week before spring break, so I had a two-week vacation from school.

On the first school day of my suspension in the middle of April, a peddler on a horse-drawn wagon passed as I was sitting outside my building. An elderly Greek immigrant named Tom Wolfe, he had a regular route through the neighborhood during the spring and summer peddling his fresh and high-quality produce around the city. He had a good reputation among his regular customers in the neighborhood, who called him only by his last name.

Kids would go through the neighborhood hawking (announcing) the sale of fruits and vegetables to get residents to go out to the wagon to buy produce. I was excited that I was the only kid on the street with the opportunity to learn how to make money delivering groceries for Tom Wolfe.

Women, including Momma, lined up to buy Wolfe's produce by the bushel.

"Do you need any help today?" I asked Wolfe between customers,

"Can you carry a bushel?" he replied in his heavily accented voice, clenching a cigar between his front teeth.

I said yes, and he handed me a half-full basket. Wolfe told me to take it to the house of the lady who just finished her purchase. When I returned to the street, Wolfe asked if my mother knew I wanted to go with him to work all day. I said she didn't, but I would go ask her.

I sprinted into the building, bounded up the two flights of stairs, flung open the door and yelled to my mother, "Can I go work with Mr. Wolfe today?!"

"What are you talking about?" she asked.

"Tom Wolfe wants me to go with him to work today, but he wants to know if it's all right with you," I stammered.

"You can't stay out of trouble in school. How can he depend on you when you haven't shown that you can act responsibly?" she asked with earned skepticism, not expecting a response.

She walked down to the wagon to talk to Wolfe. She told him why I was out of school and instructed him to send me home the first time I acted out. I believed she thought I would learn self-respect and discipline. Like that, I got my first job.

I was paid fifty cents for about four hours of work on my first day. At the end of the route, which covered a three- to five-mile radius from my neighborhood, Wolfe told me, "If you want to work tomorrow, meet me at 35th and LaSalle as I start my route at 7 a.m. If you're not there on time, I can't use you."

I left early to walk the three blocks from my house and arrive at that corner on time the next day and every day for the rest of the summer and the following one. Fifty cents a day progressed to a dollar a day and a dollar and a half on Saturdays, Wolfe's big business day. I learned a lot about responsibility, dependability, honesty, and integrity during the summers I worked with Wolfe. After I made deliveries, he allowed me to collect and return payments for sales when often it was not clear what the costs of the products were before the customers made choices. More than anything else, I realized the importance of discipline in conducting myself in ways that would not cause me to lose my cool.

When I was fourteen, I got an itch to get a full-time job. I had a chance to work a few days during the summer with an older "cousin," (Black vernacular for a family friend) who had a summer job in a small downtown eatery.

The son of one of my mother's high school classmates in Fairfield, Alabama, Adam Jr. was like a big brother to me. He was an excellent student and musician at Fairfield

Industrial High School – alma mater of Major League Baseball Hall of Famer Willie Mays. Adam Jr. went to the historically Black Dillard University in New Orleans. He came to Chicago and stayed at our house during the summers to earn money for college.

He had been the dishwasher and became the short order cook. Summer employment opportunities were scarce for Black college students in the South in the 1950s. He wanted to hold his dishwasher position open until his classmate, who needed a summer job, could take a train to Chicago in a couple days. Until he arrived, I'd be his stand-in. I worked for two days, enough time for me to get excited about finding a regular hourly job. During the summer I had the opportunity to work with Adam Jr. – while holding open a summer job for his classmate, Thomas Dubose. Both men were a positive force in my life that helped me realize that I could graduate from college as they had done.

I was determined to find a full-time job the next summer and didn't have a clue how to go about it. After learning about large businesses' employment offices, I went to a downtown Chicago department store and requested an application for a job as a stock boy because I had heard that was the kind of full-time job available to high school students for the summer.

I then watched the receptionist, who made no attempt at subtlety as she put my completed application card on the bottom of the pile. Unsurprisingly, I didn't get a chance to talk to anyone about a job that day. I looked around in other department stores, never seeing any Black teenagers working as stock boys in any of them. I decided to take a different approach.

With my brief experience the previous summer as a stand-in dishwasher, I went from restaurant door to restaurant door asking at the front desks if they needed any help. My new approach was just as unsuccessful as the old.

One morning, I decided to walk through a downtown alley behind Clark Street, a major commercial artery in the Loop. As I passed an open back door leading into a big, busy and brightly lit kitchen, I saw a portly man with a ruddy complexion, wearing a white shirt and tie over a black apron folded down to his waist. As he stood in the doorway smoking a cigarette, I overheard him giving instructions to two young dark skinned guys not much older than I.

When he looked like he was finished talking to the two men, I approached the door and as I felt a hot breeze coming from the kitchen I said, "Excuse me sir?"

"Yea, what do you want?" He turned and replied, as if he expected a request for food or something.

"Do you need any help today?" I asked quickly, just as I had to Wolfe so many years earlier.

"Can you work nights?"

I felt a sense of excitement as I replied affirmatively. The man took one last drag on his cigarette, flicked it away, inhaled, and said come back tonight at 11:30.

I thanked him. I didn't know how much money I'd be paid or what working all night would be like, but I was excited about the possibility of getting to work full-time.

I wasn't sure of where I was, so I went around the corner to the front of the building to get the name of the restaurant. It was Toffenetti's, one in a chain of downtown eateries that had been in Chicago for decades. It was a mid-priced, linen tablecloth service establishment before fast food came into vogue. Toffenetti's featured an Italian menu emphasizing spaghetti and meat sauce, ham and sweet potatoes, freshly baked biscuits for strawberry shortcake during the summer months, and pots upon pots of freshly brewed coffee.

I went back at 11:30 that night and the tall middle-aged blonde female night manager met me at the front desk. She handed me a heavy white cotton apron, a paper hat and a three by nine-inch index card employment application as she uttered an inquiry.

"Can you write?"

I immediately stiffened with a feeling of insult at the implication that I was illiterate.

"Yes, I can write," I mumbled with a sullen attitude.

I took the card, and in my most careful cursive wrote my responses to each question. I was so eager to contradict what I perceived as her assumption I was a dummy, that I didn't read the instructions written in bold capital letters, "PLEASE PRINT." She accepted the card anyway.

When I finished the application, she and I walked through the dimly lit, long narrow dining-car-like room. Chairs were stacked upside down in sets of four, on top of a double row of tables lining each side of the room. We continued down a set of winding wooden stairs to a hot, humid large open space. She called out, "Willie?"

Willie emerged with a limp from behind a high stack of metal boxes full of unwashed dishes and silverware. A heavy-set dark complexioned balding man, in his fifties, said in a recognizable South Side cadence, "Youngblood gonna bus dishes tonight?" The manager nodded.

Things were slow after midnight. I sat on a bench at the foot of the stairs between runs and nodded drowsily. I had never stayed up all night away from home and surely not doing something like working. It seemed like every time I dozed off, I heard a booming baritone voice calling, "Youngblood!"

Willie had a padded chair behind the dishwasher where he sat most of the night as he directed me where and how I should stack the dirty dishware.

"Youngblood, you need to arrange the dishes in different piles, put the silverware in this tumbling washing machine and put the racks of dirty glasses in the glass washing machine," he said.

At that point, I realized I was also Willie's helper. He sat down most of the night and began to get busy just before daybreak, when I experienced a second wind.

When I returned the next day, the manager told me I was being transferred to another Toffenetti's about three blocks west on Madison. The Madison Street location was a smaller and more elegant facility with wood-paneled wainscoting and deep green tablecloths under four sets of white cotton napkins and silverware on each table.

The restaurant was on the edge of the city's financial district and three blocks east of Chicago's Civic Opera House. Its neighbors were commercial businesses and high-end men's fashion boutiques. Daily, I observed elegantly dressed men having lunch and discussing business. I heard people leaving concerts and performances at the Civic Opera House discuss their feelings about the arts while enjoying desserts and coffee.

Even though I had a menial job, the neighborhood around the restaurant provided exposure to experiences I'd never have seen at my age had I not ventured away from the South Side. In later years, those glimpses became my motivation to keep striving for success no matter what obstacles I encountered. Because of the menial nature of some jobs or how we tend to regard people doing such work, some young people from low-income backgrounds like mine may not appreciate the opportunity to expand their horizons when in circumstances like washing dishes in a restaurant. I learned that a menial job doesn't define a person or that person's aspirations.

"One thing you can say about Phillip is that he has learned to work" became my mother's refrain. I was fortunate she gave me the opportunity to develop a sense of independence and responsibility from the time I blew it in the fourth grade until I reached the threshold of adulthood.

Based on the premise that we are products of our environments, it is reasonable to conclude that children from stable two-parent families with economic resources and sound educational backgrounds are advantaged and more likely to succeed educationally and economically. That was not my environment, which lacked the educational and economic advantages of solid middle-class communities.

However, as I think about my experiences growing up, I realize my environment consisted of more than my immediate family and neighborhood. My development involved a series of interrelated experiences in a variety of situations and different environments that created many opportunities for me to learn outside the classroom and my immediate surroundings. Much of my learning occurred on the street in the school of hard knocks.

Privileged children learn while they are in and out of school, while poor children may be disadvantaged when it comes to learning such fundamentals as reading and mathematics outside of school. Silas Purnell, who ran a successful Talent Search program at the Ada S. McKinley Educational Center in Chicago's Dearborn Housing Project from the 1960s until the 1990s, would refer to this learning advantage as the result of "17 years of dinner conversation."

I was fortunate my childhood included positive values strong enough to overcome my neighborhood's inherent disadvantages. I learned that every experience can be a good experience if you learn something from it. I learned to value striving to succeed despite the temptations of the street. In the inner city, the street always takes its toll. I learned the parable "Raise a child in the way he should go, and he will not stray far from it." Luck has been described as preparation and opportunity. I guess I got lucky in this regard.

****

I, like many Black boys my age, had the images of Jackie Robinson, Joe Louis and Jesse Owens impressed upon me by adults and society as Black men of great accomplishment. Paul Robeson, Phi Beta Kappa scholar, singer, actor, athlete, and social activist, was a man my mother held up to me as a person of integrity to emulate. I once had an opportunity to hear him speak and sing at our church. His voice was magnificent as it shook the rafters of the building.

My Sunday school teacher Mr. Flowers was the first of many male role models in my life. A small man who made his living as a restaurant cook and wore long graying locks swept back from his forehead, he was the scout master of my church's Boy Scouts troop. In his quiet way, Mr. Flowers exuded a sense of serious honor and authority without being militaristic. He demonstrated his ability to encourage excellence by preparing three Eagle Scouts during his tenure before I was old enough to be a scout. In our neighborhood, that was quite an accomplishment. Mr. Flowers never told you to be a certain way. He would stop what he was saying or doing when we were not paying attention and his demeanor communicated quite convincingly that he didn't approve of our behavior.

Mr. Flowers quizzed his Sunday school students on each day's lesson and for every correct answer you gave, you moved up in the line of chairs to the head of the classroom when someone ahead of you answered incorrectly. I spent a lot of time at the front of the line because I liked the game so much I always studied the Sunday school lesson before class because I enjoyed Bible stories.

As the scout master, Mr. Flowers showed his confidence in me by appointing me senior patrol leader while I had only achieved second-class scouting rank while the basic requirement for senior patrol leader is first-class rank. Mr. Flowers thought I had leadership potential and that the senior patrol appointment would encourage me to achieve first-class rank. I participated in Boy Scouts for about two years and learned to feel confident in my leadership abilities, but I never reached first-class rank because I quit scouting to earn money selling newspapers before night games and Sunday doubleheaders at Comiskey Park.

Through folk sayings like, "When you earn a dollar, save a dime," Pa Dallas – a barber who along with his wife Aunt Cael provided housing for my mother when she first came to Chicago – gave me grounding in "mother-wit," known outside of Black vernacular as basic common sense. He and Aunt Cael helped take care of my sister and me after my mother, homeless after leaving Gary, Indiana, arrived in Chicago.

Pa Dallas' sayings comprise a cultural legacy – characterized by Albert Murray, as blues idiom – passed to me and my generational peers by older Black people who were southern migrants with many life experiences but little formal education.

As a teenager, the hip dudes in the community became my male role models. They were always sharp, dressed to the nines in cool slacks and shirts, highly shined Stacy Adams shoes with white outer-sole stitching and Dobbs hats worn cocked to one side. These men were generally regarded as good athletes, talked a good game and thought they were favored by the girls.

I followed two articulate and friendly guys, Less and Leroy. Both were three or four years older than I. As a senior in high school, I happened upon Less after not having seen him for a long time. Gone were the neat stylish clothes I'd admired. His eyes were glassy. His speech was slow and stammering. Less was strung out on drugs. I cried, afraid this could happen to me.

Leroy didn't have a drug problem. He was a wino who could usually be found hanging out at a neighborhood tavern drinking "pluck" (cheap wine) and debating deep subjects like defining the "ifness in why."

Neither Less nor Leroy finished high school. They were unemployed. Leroy had an unhealthy reddish-brown complexion because of his drinking and had lost most of his teeth. Less' hands, arms and swollen ankles bore the marks of repeated needle injections. They looked much older than four years my senior. I felt a sense of loss and helplessness to do something about their conditions. At that point, I knew I wanted to do something to keep the street from taking its toll on so many guys in my neighborhood.

When it came to biological relatives, though, the women had the greatest influence on my young life. My mother was the center of my universe and her sister, my Aunt Jessie, was a strict person with a soft heart. A unique woman for her era, Aunt Jessie was unmarried and an entrepreneur. She sold Madam C.J. Walker beauty products for Black women from the back of her 1940s style Plymouth automobile from Gary to the South Side.

I remember her as a small woman with a big voice. She wore glasses and a monocle for reading to compensate for the effects of her diabetes. Upfront about her illness, to say the least, Aunt Jessie would openly raise her skirt to inject her insulin. She eventually lost her eyesight and a leg before she died.

At a gathering after her funeral, my mother told me quietly to get my coat and come outside with her. She didn't say anything as we walked out into the cold winter night air. I wondered where we were going and what we were doing, but I didn't ask. We walked about a block to where a car was parked with the engine running and the headlights turned off. Momma went up to the car and said something to the driver. She beckoned me to join her as she opened the front door.

I slid over on the velvety brown bench seat with the floor gearshift between me and the driver. She got in, sat next to me, and told the driver to find a bright spot to park. We drove a short distance and parked under a streetlight.

"Before your Aunt Jessie died, I promised her I would do this for you," Momma said to me. "Before you were born, I lived with my sister Jessie and she knew who your father is. Son, this is John Seals. He's your father."

I had often wondered about what my father looked like, and I think my surroundings made it easy to suppress concerns about it because fatherless homes were a frequent occurrence – if not yet the norm in my community.

I didn't feel surprised or disappointed. I was numb. I didn't spend time anticipating meeting him.

I turned slightly to my left to see a broad woolen newsboy style cap above an oval-shaped clean-shaven face in the shadows. His expression was blank. He didn't speak immediately.

"See how you have similar pointed noses and cheek bones and look at your eyes – they're just alike," Momma continued.

"Yes, I'm your father," he spoke in a quiet tone. "I did see you when you were born. Your mother and I decided that it would be best not to say anything to my family or her family and she has taken care of you ever since."

I associated the event with the loss of my aunt and recognized the experience as something significantly related to her passing. I needed time and distance to absorb the meaning of the meeting.

While ordinarily it didn't matter when I was growing up, there was an occasion when I reacted to not having a father. I was listening to Christmas carols on the radio one Christmas Eve, when a song by Nat "King" Cole came on. He sang the lyrics, "…He's the little boy that Santa Claus forgot. I'm so sorry for that laddy, he hasn't got a daddy. He's the little boy that Santa Clause forgot." My vision of the lights on our Christmas tree blurred as tears dripped to my chest. I became overcome by a great feeling of melancholy. I wasn't conscious of the sentiment expressed in the song at that time and didn't understand my emotional reaction. I felt alone and lonely, something I'd never knowingly experienced before.

I didn't see John Seals again for more than two decades. I was grown, finished college, married, and had our first child, Phyllis. Momma believed in the importance of family lineage. She wanted me to introduce my daughter to her grandfather. Momma arranged everything. She took my wife, Jo, new baby Phyllis, and me to John Seals' house in Gary. It was a small, aged, rundown bungalow in an older part of town. He lived alone. His wife had died several years earlier, and I was told they had no children.

I was startled by the impact of seeing my father for the first time in the daylight, in a real-life situation, and in regular street clothes. I reacted emotionally to the physical cues I recognized in him that reminded me of myself. His stature and mine were similar. He was in his late sixties with a clean-shaven head, a broad barrel chest and solid frame. My attention was drawn to the wide palms and long fingers of his hands that were a mirror image of my own. Our faces were similar, and he had remarkably smooth facial features for his age. I'd never had such a feeling of familiarity and identity with another person. In that moment, I wasn't the little boy that Santa Claus forgot.

Memories of that teary Christmas Eve contributed to my desire to be a father someday. Subconsciously, I wanted to fill a void in my life by being the father for my children that I never had. An electric train I received that Christmas Eve became my symbol for that experience. It was a replica of the old Lionel steam engine freight train with a red caboose. I was so proud of that train and enjoyed it so much that I put it around the Christmas tree every year after I got it until I went away to college.

I passed my Lionel train on to my son, Joel. Annually when he was growing up, we went to an antique train dealer in Cedar Rapids, Iowa, to find parts for my old electric train. By the time Joel was a teenager, we had amassed another complete old Lionel steam engine train. The next link in this family tradition has been established now that my grandchildren, Joel's son Kennedy and daughter Lola, have the original Lionel electric train.

Chapter Two:

"Nothing Beats a Failure But a Try"

My high school experience was quite different than elementary school. Tilden Technical High School was an all-male college preparatory high school. Students, selected by entry examinations, came from diverse ethnic and racial South Side communities – and it was said that only one in every four applicants gained admission. Most students were Irish, Polish, and Italian with significant minor representations of Chinese, Latino and Black students.

I played football for four years with some involvement in track and wrestling along the way. My academic performance and athletic participation were ordinary. Although I was a starter as a sophomore on the freshman-sophomore team and earned two varsity letters as a junior and senior in football, I was never a starter on the varsity team. My graduating class had about seventy-five students and I finished in the upper two-thirds.

I graduated from high school in January,1959. I wanted to go to college, but I wasn't sure what I wanted to study. Like many youngsters then and now, I had no idea about choosing a major. I dreamed of being a physician but had no confidence I was smart enough to do that. I thought I'd like to study physical education, but was dissuaded by a counselor who told me, "That's a major for washed-up jocks." I didn't want to think of myself as a washed-up jock, so I chose something else. After talking to a classmate who had similar ideas, we both decided to apply to the University of Illinois College of Pharmacy, in Chicago. I didn't know anything about pharmacy, but it seemed like a good idea at the time.

My classmate and I were admitted for the fall of 1959. Because I had to sit out during the spring semester, to get a head start I decided to enroll at Wilson Junior College, now Kennedy-King College, on the South Side. My scores on math and English placement exams placed me in basic college algebra and introductory English composition classes. I didn't mind because I didn't feel strong in either subject.

I took German because I heard German was required for pharmacy. Not true, but I didn't know any better, and I didn't have any academic advising. Misguided, I got off to a poor start. I didn't know how to study. My basic math skills were lacking. I didn't know basic grammar for writing, and I had no idea about foreign language study since I had not taken a foreign language in high school. I struggled but managed to earn a "C" average.

In September, I started at the College of Pharmacy on the University of Illinois Medical Campus in Chicago. Once again, I had a poor start. Every morning, I started my commute to school with a tight feeling in my chest and stomach.

My high school was predominantly white and all male. Wilson Junior College students were diverse age, gender, and race/ethnicity. Pharmacy school was white and predominantly male. I felt alone and out of place. I didn't know anybody. I learned quickly that pharmacy students study together. I lived at home and studied alone. I had very low self-confidence.

I realized I didn't have the level of skills required for the course. Mother told me, "If you're having trouble learning and don't enjoy what you're doing, maybe you should do something different. There's no shame in admitting you've made a mistake when you've put forth your best effort. Do something different that you can succeed in, and always put forth your best effort. Nothing beats a failure but a try." I've given this same advice to many students during my career.

After three weeks I withdrew from pharmacy school. Complete withdrawal was necessary because the pharmacy school was on a quarter calendar and the two-year branch of the University of Illinois at Navy Pier in Chicago was on a semester schedule, so I had to wait until the beginning of spring semester 1960 to enroll in the physical education program.

During the interim, I sought psychological counseling for the tension and depression I felt in pharmacy school. I learned that I had a case of anxiety neurosis which went away after I withdrew from pharmacy school.

I found a part-time job at the Newberry Library, an internationally recognized private humanities library. Book stacks were closed to the public, so staff pages were used to get and return books for use. The Newberry is a fascinating place I had heard about from a high school friend who had worked there before going into the military. I wondered if his position had been filled so I went to inquire.

When I arrived at the library, I met and talked to Mr. Bowman, the assistant librarian. I asked him if there was an opening for a page position. No permanent page position was available, but he said he needed someone for a temporary job for two or three nights.

When I returned that evening for my four-hour shift, I was taken to the hot and humid basement occupied by a large group of huge volumes that smelled of wet paper and leather bindings. Right away, I thought I knew why the job required temporary help; no one on the permanent staff wanted to do it.

The gig turned out to be a blessing in disguise. The walls and floors of the room were soaked, so I had to move the large sets of century-old annually accumulated volumes of periodicals and newspapers – such as the Manchester Guardian, London Times and Punch – about fifty feet to a large wide wooden stack of shelves in a dry section of the basement.

Dissolved, deteriorated leather covered the arms of my jacket and across the apron I had been given for the job as I lifted the fragile documents to put them on a cart. After loading four or five of the approximately two feet wide and three feet long, ten-pound bound folios onto the cart–that rumbled like a railroad boxcar, I pushed it across the floor to a new set of stacks in a dry area of the basement. There were thirty to forty folios in the set. I completed the task in two and a half nights. On the last evening Mr. Bowman had a librarian begin orienting me to the responsibilities of serving as a page.

I was raised to believe that any job worth doing is worth doing well. I've always remembered and tried to impart that lesson to others. Doing a job nobody else wanted to do was instrumental in me receiving invaluable developmental experience so I worked part-time at Newberry while I attended Illinois at Navy Pier and full-time in the summer for a year and a half.

My enrollment at the University of Illinois at Navy Pier in 1960 coincided with the beginning of the Civil Rights Movement on college campuses in the South and social protests on predominantly white campuses in the North and West. I formed my perspective on the Movement through my daily exposure to a variety of news publications at Newberry. I also saw televised news stories showing the insults and violence against sit-in demonstrators and pickets.

At Navy Pier, groups of white students sympathetic with the developing Civil Rights Movement held meetings, organized and began to hold symbolic solidarity demonstrations. These included speeches on campus, columns in campus newspapers and ad hoc meetings of newly formed protest groups of white students. They made plans to picket Woolworth's in downtown Chicago.

For some of us Black students, that presented a dilemma: Lunch counters at Woolworth's and other five and ten stores were not segregated in Chicago, and Black people held many of the service jobs at lunch counters. We thought it wouldn't be right to demonstrate against Black workers at lunch counters in these stores. I was conflicted. I wanted to do something to support the cause, but I didn't trust the motives of the demonstration's organizers. Several other Black guys at the Pier felt the same way, but we decided to go as a group to represent our student community.

On a gray, cloudy, winter Saturday morning, a group of fifteen to twenty Black and white college students – men and women – carrying handmade signs gathered at Woolworth's on State Street and Washington Street downtown to encourage people not to shop at the store until all Woolworth's lunch counters in the South were desegregated. The irony of picketing a desegregated business in a city that had the largest de facto segregated housing and education systems of any major city outside of the South was not lost on me.

I experienced real racial discrimination in my first week at the University of Illinois in Champaign, where I transferred in fall 1961. I was assigned a double room on the first floor in Garner Hall. Men's halls were overcrowded, and some students were temporarily sleeping in floor lounges. I arrived at about noon on Sunday morning, checked in, got my key, found my room, and began to move in. My roommate had already arrived and hung his clothes in one of the closets.

As my mother and I unpacked and began to make one of the twin beds facing the window, we heard a key opening the door behind us. A tall, pleasant-looking man appeared from the shadows. He looked up to see my mother and me. Before we could say a word, blood seemed to drain from his suntanned face. He pivoted toward the closet door on the right side of the room adjacent to the room door, locked it, turned and left the room closing the door behind him wordlessly. At that moment I learned a lesson from my mother that I've never forgotten.

"Don't worry about that," she said. "You're paying rent on half of this room. Live in your half and respect whoever lives in the other half."

I met my roommate again later that night. We spoke to each other but didn't say much else the rest of the night. He constantly stared at me. When I returned to my room after breakfast the next morning, he and all his belongings were gone. Although hundreds of students were sleeping in lounges waiting for room assignments, he had been transferred to another room in the system.

Discrimination in those days was not only on campus. I had a similar experience in Champaign during my first week on campus. It was a tangible example of what many Black students experience in overt and subtle ways – then as well as now. I was walking along Wright Street, the dividing line between the twin cities of Champaign and Urbana, when I saw a sign in the window of a campus bar and grill advertising for a dishwasher. I hadn't started looking for a job, but since I had previous experience washing dishes in a restaurant, I thought I'd check it out.

As I walked through the door, a tall balding man met me immediately.

"Can I do something for you?" He said in a curt tone of voice.

"I just came in to find out about the job on the sign in the window," I replied.

He turned uncomfortably toward me and said dismissively, "I just don't want colored people in my place."

I was stunned, but I was cool although my chest swelled up and my blood pressure rose. These two lessons introduced me to the painful realities of living in a predominantly white community, one that had a few Black students and even fewer social bars or clubs welcoming to us – at least based on the music they played and food they served.

At the beginning of spring semester, I moved into the Kappa Alpha Psi house (I'd been initiated while I was a student at Navy Pier.) As the only Black fraternity house on campus, there were strong feelings of togetherness and understanding of the cultural and economic differences between us and our white Greek counterparts. We lived racially segregated and socially isolated existences on a large campus in a small predominantly white conservative central Illinois community. Downstate Illinois was sometimes characterized as "up South" in terms of racial attitudes.

I was elected to the leadership of the chapter, first as secretary and later as house president. As president, I attended the Inter-Fraternity Council (IFC) meetings. A time prior to the passage of the Civil Rights Act of 1964, white male and female social fraternal organizations debated about exclusionary clauses in many of their constitutions that restricted membership to white gentiles.

Passage of the Civil Rights Act prohibited racial and religious discrimination among social fraternities and sororities in colleges and universities receiving federal funds. Discussions in the IFC meetings were hotly contested assertions among the white Greeks about losing their rights to free association. The act barred racial discrimination in Greek letter organizations' admissions practices, but social isolation and racial separation remain traditions in fraternities and sororities to this day.

The Black Greek organizations, comprising a population of 100 or fewer students, maintained an active calendar of events outside mainstream Greek social life. The one Black fraternity and two Black sorority chapter houses were often venues for social events for all Black students regardless of Greek affiliation. To avoid confusion in scheduling events, the three Black Greek organizations decided to develop a set of guidelines to coordinate our gatherings. The president of the Delta Sigma Theta sorority house, a bright and articulate honor student, and I were charged to develop the guidelines.

She was a math major with a great personality from Decatur, Illinois, south of Chicago. Her name was Jo Lavera Kennedy. We were both juniors when we met. We dated during the rest of our undergraduate years. We both graduated in 1963 and married in January 1964, a union that continues to this day.

Living on campus forced me to learn to manage my time better. I was used to needing two hours to get to school and to class on time as a commuting student in the city. Despite the admonition from the high school counselor, I majored in physical education (PE). The College of Physical Education was about a half a block away in Huff Gym where my morning classes were held. Invariably, I would underestimate how much time I needed to finish my meal-service job in the mornings, return to my room, and get to class on time.

It was easy to procrastinate and then not have sufficient time to prepare for class. PE majors were required to take the same anatomy lecture and laboratory course as pre-med students. Anatomy, which met five days a week, was considered a flunk out course for a lot of guys in PE – especially athletes. I enjoyed anatomy but didn't have proper study habits to excel. A significant part of lab work in beginning anatomy is rote memory, but interpretive learning is essential for understanding and explaining the interrelations and interactions of human systems. At that point as a college student, I didn't understand the importance of overlearning. I dropped the course, but I later retook and passed it. I learned a valuable lesson about studying that I taught to many students during my career: "Every hour in class requires two hours' preparation outside of it."

As graduation approached, I thought of many things I'd like to do to make a difference in society. Through my interactions as a leader of the fraternity and my association with Jo, I'd begun to recognize and understand the importance of participating in social change through organized development. I'm sure I was no different than many others about to finish college then or now. "Freedom Now" was a theme of the Civil Rights Movement, and the charismatic President John F. Kennedy had given my generation the challenge to "Ask not what your country can do for you, but what you can do for your country." Many college men graduating in 1963 had selective service deferments from being drafted into military service. This was before the escalation of the draft for the war in Vietnam.

Registration for the draft was always a mystery to me. Unlike many of my Black classmates and practically everyone in my fraternity, I had never been called by my draft board about my 1-A status or to take a physical exam. Many of my Kappa brothers were drafted. I was out of college before I realized a possible rationale for my good fortune.

My draft board was not in Bronzeville. It was on the southwest side in Bridgeport near the Chicago Stock Yards. My high school was about a half mile from the Stock Yards and my draft board was in the Stock Yard Inn at 43rd and Halsted Street.

The Bridgeport neighborhood was where the Chicago mayors, Richard J. Daley and Richard M. Daley, lived. My draft board seemed to give preference to white men in college living in the area, and my name may have been considered among them. There may not have been many other Blacks in college registered within my draft board. White college men registered with my draft board, or those assumed to be white, may have had a disproportionate advantage over Black college men registered with an all-Black draft board. This may be why a disproportionate number of Blacks served in Vietnam. Whatever the case may have been I, unlike my peers, didn't have to worry about the draft as graduation approached.

Despite my good fortune, I did consider military service as a career choice, but I couldn't find an area of training that interested me and that I could transfer to civilian life. I also considered joining the Peace Corps. I was inspired by the example of Rafer Johnson, the Olympic decathlon goal medalist and UCLA graduate, who served in and endorsed the Peace Corps. I wanted to do something to give back to my community and I wanted to get married after graduation. Jo also wanted to go someplace where we both could become involved in advancing civil rights in society.

Jo graduated in May 1963 and I finished in August after completing an exercise therapy internship at the Veterans Administration Hospital in Danville, Illinois. I applied for jobs, including positions in social services and substitute teaching, in Chicago. Based on a phone call connection from my mother, I got an interview with the Chicago Youth Centers at the Lower North Center in the infamous Cabrini-Green Homes on the north side. I was hired as a group work counselor to work with boys from ages 8 through 18 in the projects and surrounding community.

The areas known as Old Town and Lincoln Park were adjacent to the projects to the north with the Chicago River west of the neighborhood and the Chicago Gold Coast immediately to the east. In 1963 the Cabrini-Green area, now called River North, was experiencing gentrification that culminated in the complete demolition of Cabrini-Green and replacement with mixed-income housing developments by the end of the century.

My work day generally spanned from noon until 10 p.m. The center opened at 3 p.m. for young people after school let out. The exercise therapy internship piqued my interest in physical therapy school, so I anticipated my job at Lower North would be short term. Physics and chemistry were prerequisites for physical therapy certificate programs. I needed both courses to qualify for admission. Once again, I signed up at Wilson Junior College to prepare for my next educational step. I left home at about 7 a.m. to go to class before work.

Soon after the school year began in September, tragedy hit the Lower North community. One Saturday night at the corner of Division and Sedgwick Streets, across from the iconic Cooley High, a young man who frequented the center was stabbed to death. Another young man who was in one of my teen youth groups was accused of the stabbing. A group of young men were hanging out and drinking wine on the corner when an argument started between two of them. After the stabbing, the guys ran in different directions – leaving the victim lying in a pool of his own blood. No one called for help and the young man bled to death before a passerby discovered him.

The youngster charged with a capital offense was one of my club members. He was an only son being raised by a single mother – which personally resonated with me. She could not afford a lawyer, nor did she know how to get legal assistance. The chairman of the board for the Chicago Youth Centers was an attorney. He agreed to represent the young man for no charge if someone from Lower North Center would gather witnesses to be interviewed for the young man's defense. Since he was in one of my clubs, I was given the task. There was insufficient evidence to hold my club member for a capital crime. The victim accidentally lost his life because of an unfortunate street corner incident.

This incident became part of a frustrating pattern of events I experienced trying to create positive change in an inner-city community I knew well because it is where I came from. My feelings were reinforced that the street always takes its toll. However, I still felt I had to keep on pushing.

Toward the end of my year at Lower North Jo and I decided that since I was spending so much time away from home every day and night between taking a class and working, it would be better for me to concentrate on getting into a physical therapy program rather than continue living and working at a rate that was not productive for my career goal nor for nourishing her creative talents.

Jo was new to Chicago. Her life was narrowly circumscribed. We didn't have a car, so she had limited mobility, walking to the few stores in our quiet South Side neighborhood. She had no opportunity to utilize her considerable talent and training in her field of teaching math education.

I resigned my position at the end of May and we made plans to return to Champaign to get part-time jobs, so I could take the physical therapy courses I needed at the University of Illinois. Jo returned to a job she had in a physics lab working on a bubble-chamber experiment. We rented a small apartment in a house in Urbana about four blocks from the campus and the physics building. I found a part-time job in the biology building washing glassware in the microbiology lab of Professor Sol Spiegleman, a pioneer in the development of processes to synthesize DNA.

I completed basic inorganic chemistry during the summer session and enrolled in organic chemistry for the fall. As I delved into the course, I experienced the same bricklike feeling in my stomach I had in pharmacy school. My limited math background put me at a disadvantage in interpreting basic organic chemistry concepts. Jo graduated with a Bachelor of Science degree in math education and she helped me. I realized I might be better off in graduate school in a field I enjoyed and for which I had strong academic preparation. Once again, Momma was right: "Do something different that you can succeed in, and always put forth your best effort. Nothing beats a failure but a try."

I had applied to several physical therapy programs, including one at the University of Iowa. I wrote to Iowa's Graduate College and requested to have my application considered for the masters' program in physical education. I learned Iowa had a strong program in exercise physiology and adapted physical education, and the women's department had leading faculty Gladys Scott and Margaret Fox in basic skill development for children – a field of study that interested me. Unlike my applications for physical therapy, I was accepted into the master's program in physical education at the University of Iowa without questions and within a short turnaround time.

Chapter Three:

The Flint Experience

G raduate school was a two-year period of introspection leading to awakenings of a heightened sense of family connection, adult responsibility, social awareness and an expanded appreciation for art, music, and literature. These epiphanies occurred against a backdrop of social revolution with respect to the war in Vietnam and human rights around the world.

There was upheaval in my family life. One month before I finished my master's degree in 1967, my older sister Frankie, who was eighteen months older than I, died from a cerebral hemorrhage at the age of twenty-seven. Although both our last names were Jones, we had different fathers. She was born in Gary, Indiana. I was born in Chicago, Illinois. She maintained contact with her father's family in Gary while we grew up and I didn't. We experienced separation as teens when she had two children after finishing high school. She left a ten- year- old son and a nine-year-old daughter. I considered adopting them before my mother decided to keep them in Chicago with her.

Jo and I also became parents of a daughter, Phyllis Lavera. I began to think seriously about what I should do with my life in terms of how to balance becoming a good father and being a person with a strong commitment to creating social change while at the same time keeping a job and advancing my career.

When I felt restless, I'd go for walks to talk to myself about my thoughts and dreams.

"I don't know what I'm going to do, but whatever it is, I'm going to do something to make things better," was my common refrain. Making that vow to myself brightened my surroundings and eased my being.

I applied for teaching positions in several midwestern cities. I wrote to the Flint, Michigan, school district because it seemed to have strong physical education programs and advertised for an athletic trainer, a position I held in spring training with the 1964 Rose Bowl winning Fighting Illini football team and the outdoor track team during my year after returning to Champaign. The district offered me the position, which included teaching physical education and psychology, at Flint Northern High School.

My experiences during that year in Flint defined me to some in the community as a militant activist, though I'd never applied those descriptors to myself.

Flint was largely a working-class manufacturing union town, home to General Motors' Buick corporate headquarters, the country's second largest foundry, and other automotive suppliers. Many Buick workers both Black and white were migrants from the south, and some were transitory between southern states and Flint, when auto production slowed. As racially diverse as Flint was, its downtown housed a presidential campaign office for infamous segregationist Alabama Governor George C. Wallace – indicative of the city's political atmosphere.

Many "For Sale" signs dotting block after block on the city's north side made it clear this was a community in racial transition. Jo and I with baby Phyllis in tow rented a small house a mile from Flint Northern High School. Our home was located on White Street, west of Detroit Street – the red-lining housing boundary between Black and white communities. Black residents were moving further west, and the community was experiencing white flight.

Those changing demographics led to tensions between the schools and Flint's Black residents. Being new in town, I had not directly experienced the atmosphere. However, it was not difficult to discern that there were tensions based on the changing demographics of the community surrounding Northern High School. In response, school board administrators held a school and community retreat before classes started in fall 1967.

Soon after the facilitators opened the first session, the Brougham Club – several young Black men sporting various styles of beards and skull caps and dressed in dashikis — raised questions about the gathering's relevance and presented a series of demands they believed the school administrators should address about community control of schools, particularly regarding the treatment of Black males.

The demographic divisions in the room were evident: The Northern teaching staff was equally comprised of men and women, but the diversity stopped there. All the administrators were male and all but one was white. In contrast to the school's community most of the teachers were white. Most of the parents were Black women.

The facilitators were unable to get the sides to reach an accord. The administrators sat passively as members of the Brougham Club shouted tirades. The administrators assembled near the door before disappearing wordlessly. Facilitators divided the remaining teachers, parents, and other community members into discussion groups. Everyone moved awkwardly throughout the room trying to shield themselves from the impending truths about to emerge in conversations about how race is lived in America. My group's facilitator seemed unsure of how to open the conversation.

I sensed an uncomfortable restlessness among the group. The facilitator directed specific questions to us about our feelings for improving understanding and communications among teachers, administrators, and parents in the community. No one contradicted the controversy raised by the Broughams until I questioned the premise that teachers and administrators were racially biased and the administrators' lack of response to explain their position.

I felt awkward sitting silently, so I spoke up, "It seems to me that there's a responsibility on both sides to respect the students and their parents on one hand, but also to support the teachers to hold students accountable for their behavior while expecting them to achieve high standards, and the teachers need to avoid discrimination by patronization." My comment defused some of the tension in the room.

The white members of the group began to raise their downcast eyes and showed more interest in having a conversation. The facilitator was able to generate meaningful discussion and a list of issues for the next large group session.

After the retreat, some participating north side parents asked me to meet in the community for confidential discussions about their views of how their children were being treated in school. I was surprised when a parent of one of my physical education students asked an assistant principal to include me to increase her trust in a conference about her son's behavior. I had cordial relationships with some white teachers, but, overall, I encountered passive resistance from most of them. Black teachers didn't raise issues about racial attitudes among their white counterparts and administrators. I did not have an open relationship to share the parents' views with my colleagues.

As a new teacher, I received a schedule with an open first period for hall monitoring and covering for absent teachers before regular substitutes arrived. As I made my rounds each morning, I frequently noticed Black male students – who, as they often do, stood out among the white majority – going into the boys' restroom after the first bell rang. Finally, one morning I followed them and asked, "Why are you guys in the bathroom during classes?"

A student I knew from one of the teams I worked with spoke up.

"Doc Jones," he said using a nickname his teammates had dubbed me within the training room, "The teachers lock us out when the bell rings."

"Why were you late for class in the first place?" I countered.

"I work nights and it's hard for me to get up for school at 8 o'clock in the morning," one guy said, initiating a cascade of excuses. Others blamed the teachers for what they perceived as prejudice against the Black male students. I was surprised to learn there were high school boys working full-time at the Buick plants. I explained I understood their feelings but impressed the importance of showing a responsible attitude and the value of putting forth their best effort to do well in school.

Incensed that my colleagues would show so little sensitivity to students' needs, and unaware that Michigan state law forbade students from being excluded from class for trivial reasons, I confronted the predominantly white teaching staff during the next teachers' meeting. I shared how those students felt about being locked out. No one said a word. I felt vindicated for what I believed explained the students' behavior.

When I got home that night, I recounted the incident triumphantly to my wife. Jo listened quietly and looked thoughtfully off into the distance.

"What did you accomplish?" She asked peacefully.

I was stunned. That wasn't the reaction I wanted. I reacted defensively and argumentatively before she calmly repeated her question. I knew what she meant, but I didn't want to admit I was wrong to castigate the teachers rather than discuss the students' behavior civilly and suggest alternatives to correct their behaviors. From Jo I learned it is more important to win than simply to raise hell, a lesson that served me well throughout my career.

Each Friday I hosted an open forum in my psychology classes emphasizing the connections between the basic terminology of psychology, societal conditions, and my students' lives. I had gained acceptance among the seniors in my class to the extent that they asked me to serve as one of the senior class' two faculty sponsors. I agreed and worked with the soon-to-be-graduates on a community car wash project and a dance.

Controversy arose about casting for the senior class play. A Black female student auditioned for and earned the lead role in the play opposite a white male. In response, a teacher supplanted her with a white student. As a result, she incited an uproar from students of both races.

Without telling me, my students made the casting controversy a topic for our Friday seminar and invited others to attend. Once the bell rang before my first psychology class of the afternoon, students lined the entire length of the twenty-yard hallway outside my classroom waiting to enter. The assistant principal and the school public safety officer soon arrived.

The assistant principal asked me to send the students to the cafeteria where there was more room to hold a discussion. Unlike the adults – school personnel and parents, both Black and white – who participated in the retreat at the beginning of the school year, the students openly offered their views about race relations and their disapproval of the racial casting decision for the student theater play. I had no qualms about leading the discussion, because it was essentially the type of discussion my students had in my psychology class every Friday.

My cordial relations with other teachers and coaches continued. Most were careful to avoid controversial issues with me, although there were times I'd hear insensitive or culturally derogatory comments such as, "you people" or "that's how they are." Our culture now has the language to identify those comments as micro-aggressions. Back then, those remarks were just the price of admission for trying to get along in integrated society.

I didn't realize I had a target on my back until I was summoned to the principal's office to meet with an administrator from the superintendent's office. I tried not to speculate about his reasoning. A tall, cinnamon complexioned man with salt-and-pepper gray hair rose from his chair, extended his right hand and introduced himself enthusiastically. His seeming sincerity distracted me to the point that I didn't hear his name. He began to speak in a vernacular cadence. I sensed the principal's uncomfortable body language as he retreated from the conversation.

"I've heard a lot of good things about you in the neighborhoods, but we've also heard that you are a Black militant," said the brother from downtown. "They say you wear dashikis and a Tiki God around your neck and a wild Afro."

I could finally relax. I knew what this was all about. I listened calm and expressionless while the top of my head felt like I was sitting under a sunlamp. When he paused for my response, I took a deep breath.

"As you can see, I don't have a wild Afro. As a matter of fact, I can't get my hair to grow long enough for much of an Afro at all," I explained. "I don't own a dashiki and have never worn one. I wear a suit and turtleneck every day and change clothes for my gym classes. The only thing I wear around my neck is a whistle for gym classes."

He turned from side to side in his chair and rolled the papers he held in his hands as I spoke. When I finished, he turned to the principal.

"I didn't think there was anything to the concerns, but since we've heard them more than once, I was asked to come visit with the two of you for the record," he said in standard English cadence.

Turning to face me, he said in a low tone, "Thanks for coming down to chat with me, Phil. I appreciate your contributions to the school and the students as well as to the community. I hope you're not offended by my inquiry."

"I appreciate learning how I might be affecting some people, and I will endeavor to communicate better," I responded.

As I walked away, I realized I had just experienced a tangible example of W.E.B. Du Bois' concept of dual consciousness and its effect on the lives of Black folk. Growing up, I had heard many times about two-faced people who smile in your face and stab you in the back. I had no concept that I was considered a militant on the other side of the veil. I learned early in life that feeling bitterness and hate would only diminish me. It was hard not to feel anger, but I told myself that I had only 15 minutes to be mad or feel sorry for myself before getting back to creating positive change. I repeat that adage to others when they feel imposed upon or discriminated against.

Regardless of race, some people on the faculty were helpful to me while others had little to say to me. Most of my Black colleagues communicated with me less than the several white teachers I encountered daily. Some Black teachers, like some white teachers, avoided controversial issues all year long.

Controversy did not do such a good job of avoiding us. On the night of April 4, Jerry Horcha, a fellow physical education teacher working on his master's degree at the University of Michigan's Flint campus, invited me to be a guest speaker in his educational administration class. I was talking about the Civil Rights Movement in education when someone barged into the classroom.

"Martin Luther King has been shot and killed in Memphis, Tennessee," the person said in a subdued voice.

My mouth felt dry, and my stomach and chest tightened. I was speechless. A hot flash crossed my face, and I had a sense of pain and rage as I looked at the eight or ten white men in the class. Responding in derogatory terms was my first response, but instead I quickly recognized an opportunity to teach. I felt a need for compassion. I sensed sorrow on the faces of men in the room. With a swelling in my throat and water filling my eyes, I spoke of a need for greater human understanding to make life better for our students and ourselves in Flint.

The next day, tensions in the school and community boiled over. It was a solemn Friday and many people, myself included, wore black to mourn the loss of Dr. King. Students were understandably upset. Black students from Northwestern High School were rumored to have walked out of school and headed to Northern to turn out our Black students. Our principal gathered several teachers to monitor the doors to the building in case the rumors were true.

Many students spent class time in the hallways. Students and teachers moved about in a fog. As rumors spread, teachers commented on the effects of the tragedy on Black students without considering the white students as if they were not affected. I spent hall duty talking to all students about the importance of treating each other with respect. Just before noon, a decision was made – I presume in the central office – to cancel classes for the rest of the day.

As students left, police cars appeared on the street in front of the building. The southeast exit faced the direction of many Black students' homes. I was the only teacher outside with them as a voice from a megaphone warned, "Please stay in the building. Do not come into the street."

Students' eyes widened as they flailed their arms in confusion. Teachers inside the school, unaware that the police were outside, coaxed students to leave as some tried to follow the police's instructions to return to the building. Without warning, a line of three or four officers in blue helmets wearing gas masks raised instruments that made a loud but muffled popping sound.

White smoke trails arced into the sky and came to earth with the pungent biting odor of onions and wood smoke. The teachers inside the building tried to secure the doors, trapping the students and me between the school and the police. When the doors finally opened, students fell inside coughing, crying, and gasping for air. All our clothes were filled with the odor of tear gas that lasted for hours.

To make matters worse, a group of Black teachers barricaded themselves in a locked office. Someone opened the door, looked out, saw me, and whispered, "Is it over?"

Everyone gasped at the smell in my clothes when I entered the office. The shades were drawn and the lights were off. They were as afraid of the situation as the students were, and my condition affirmed that, if you were Black, you would be subject to the same treatment from the police as the students.

Unfortunately, it was not the last time the police would converge on Northern High School and clash with Black students. Tensions climaxed in early June on the last day of the spring semester. The principal was waving his hand beckoning me to the door of my psychology classroom.

"I think we could have a problem if conditions continue to escalate outside," he said in a worried tone. "I'd like for you to go out and see if you can get some of those out there to calm down a little bit. I'd like to have things quieter when classes end since it's the end of the semester and the students are going to be excitable anyway."

My pulse quickened as my thoughts turned from teaching to assuming a street pose in my voice and mannerisms to relate to whoever was outside. I had to assume they were Black, given my previous community involvement during the school year. As I started back into the classroom the principal said that a substitute would cover my class.

It was a warm, sunny afternoon, and people were beginning to enjoy summertime activities, so it was not unusual for people to be sitting on porches in the neighborhood. I went to the southeast corner exit. I was surprised to see several white male teachers. I stepped between them to leave and asked, "What's going on?" At that moment, four police officers, a lieutenant and three officers in riot gear were walking hurriedly toward the building. A police van, reminiscent of a UPS delivery truck, pulled up to the corner across from Northern. I moved quickly outside, and the police lieutenant approached me and waved his arms.

"Stay in the building," he said, raising his voice. "We don't want anyone to leave the building."

"I'm a teacher," I countered with volume. "The principal asked me to come out to try to calm things down."

"Let's try to keep things calm and listen to each other," the lieutenant responded.

"I apologize I just want to try to talk to some of the young people to get them to move away from the school," I said before he allowed me to proceed.

Perpendicular to the corner where the police van was parked, three young men stood yelling obscenities at the police. I assumed that's what the principal wanted me to address. I walked up to them and recognized one as a student from one of my gym classes.

"Hey man, cool it, so you don't get picked up by the man," I said in a friendly vernacular tone of voice. I was unaware the students had been throwing things before I arrived. "You don't have to move if you just cool it a little bit."

A great commotion started across the street in a vacant lot at the corner in front of Northern. A crowd of Black students yelled at a contingent of mostly white police officers clad in riot gear. They used long sticks to push the crowd away from the corner. I rushed over to try to keep the students safe from the baton-wielding cops.

As I approached the mass of officers and students in the vacant lot, I heard a female voice shouting, "I ain't done nothin, and I ain't got to go nowhere."

I looked in her direction and saw two blue-helmeted white officers jabbing two-foot batons into the stomach and pelvis of a teenage girl who had backed herself against a parked car.

I raised my hands above my head as I moved between the girl and the officers.

"Wait. Wait. Let me talk to her," I said to the police.

"Don't fight them. Don't fight them," I said to her.

"Get out of the way. You're going to jail," an officer yelled at me.

A loud crash rang out. An officer staggered back two steps as half a house brick fell to the ground. His helmet, inches from my head, sustained a deep gash just above his temple. The thought of the brick hitting my head instead of the policemen nauseated me. Both officers cursed before one told me I was going to jail for interfering with a lawful arrest.

Nothing about the police officer's conduct toward the student seemed lawful, but the officers handcuffed me and escorted me to the waiting police van, left, and returned with the crying girl in handcuffs.

The two of us were the only ones in the cavernous van with no place to sit or anything to hold onto while rumbling through the city streets. She was handcuffed behind her back. At the police station, I was taken through a heavy metal door up to a second landing to a caged enclosure where I was stopped in front of a four-foot-high booking desk. One of three officers observing in the dimly lit area began to pat me down from my shoulders to my ankles. He suddenly took the palm of one hand and thrust it with force upward into my crotch. Fortunately, my body was not tense, so the impact was blunt and not painful. I didn't flinch. I turned toward him with blood rushing to my head but fortunately I learned growing up not to confront the police. I didn't make an aggressive move in his direction. Instead, immediately I looked him straight in the eyes and spoke a sarcastic "thank you." He glared at me and took a deep drag on his cigarette.

An officer led me through a long windowless corridor to the cellblock. My mind wandered back to one of my mother's frequent admonitions: "You're responsible for your actions. You know the difference between right and wrong. If you go to jail, you'll be there because I'm not coming to get you."

In an environment where getting arrested was an everyday thing for Black boys, I'd made it through childhood without seeing the inside of a cell. And now, I experienced a supreme irony: I'm supposed to be a responsible professional adult and here I am in jail – just another victimized Black man.

After crossing an empty cellblock into another with bright daylight streaming through windows on one wall and cells on the opposite side of the corridor, the officer approached a cell, unlocked it, and motioned me inside.

"This is where you'll be," he murmured.

Two young Black men stood at the cell bars in the cell next to mine. I recognized them as the duo I exhorted to exit the area in front of the school; one of them tried to hit me. I caught his fist in the air. He was still intoxicated. I realized they landed here for throwing the brick that struck the police officer holding me on the vacant lot. I wondered if he meant for the brick to hit me. The thought of the guys' senseless violence angered me. They contributed to creating the situation that had caused many young people to act without purpose, putting themselves in danger of being hurt, arrested, or worse. The police officers' reaction was wrong, but so were the actions of these young Black people who attacked innocent people in passing cars – some of whom were also Black.

The sunlight didn't distract me from the feeling that I'd entered a cave. I circled slowly around the cell exploring the narrow, seat-less metal toilet bowl protruding from the center of the floor. Near the back of the cell was a three-foot-wide and six-foot-long metal slab that was obviously for sleeping but lacked a mattress, pillow, or blanket. A small water fountain projected from the wall above toilet bowl which reeked of urine. The concrete floor was painted a rust color.

My mind was in a fog. I hadn't accepted the fact that I was there or that I would remain locked up. After a period – maybe an hour – an officer appeared and unlocked the cell.

"You can come with me," he said.

My chest expanded and sank deeply with a feeling of relief. Without any idea of what was happening, I assumed I was going to be released.

The officer and I retraced our steps from the dim cellblock to the booking desk. We went through a corridor into an office occupied by a receptionist who rose from a chair as if she expected me. A sign plate on the half-closed door read "Office of the Chief of Police." The receptionist invited me to enter.

Two voices came from the room. I recognized the young Black man sitting in a chair in front of the large mahogany desk as the leader of the Brougham Club I'd seen during the tense September orientation.

The chief, wearing a white shirt and black tie with colonel insignias on his collar, was sitting behind the desk. The two men were ending a conversation when the chief offered me a chair and began to explain that the Broughams had vouched for me and their endorsement was enough for him to release me on my own recognizance.

"You'll need to show up back here at 8 a.m. for arraignment in municipal court," he directed.

"Thank you," I said. "And I want to report an officer who unnecessarily struck me between my legs when he finished patting me down." I gave him the officer's badge number.

"I'll consider it," the chief said without looking up as he wrote something down.

The next day, June 6, 1968, an article about the incident ran in the Flint Journal with the headline, "Tear Gas Used by Police on Crowd Near Northern."

I was somber, but relieved to be going home. Jo was concerned but cool and supportive when I walked through the front door and picked up our one-year old daughter Phyllis. Francis Bentley – the science teacher and wrestling coach I assisted – had told Jo I had been arrested. Her first instinct was to laugh out loud to relieve her anxiety. She found my situation ironic and humorous, as she remembered what I had told her about my mother's attitude regarding me ever going to jail.

Francis told Jo that the teachers' union was providing me a lawyer and a bail bondsman to secure my release. I was reassured. I felt abandoned by the school system. I wouldn't have been outside the building had the principal not asked me to go out there.

In all the excitement, I had not thought about the fact that this would be my last day teaching at Northern because I had accepted a new position at the University of Iowa.

After an anxious night, keenly aware of my appearance, I dressed in slacks, shirt, tie, and sport coat. I went to the city jail and rang a loud bell on an iron door – the same door I'd been taken through the day before. The door opened by remote control. When I stepped inside, I felt powerless and cut off from the world. I was less than a person.

I approached the booking desk. The desk sergeant directed me to a small, brightly lit, windowless room. I stood at a counter with an ink pad and sheets of heavy paper on top.

"Place each finger and thumb down on the ink pad," a voice directed. An officer took each digit and firmly placed it on individual squares on the sheet of paper with my name and a six-digit number on top of the page.

I was then directed to a place in front of a blank white section of wall under a set of lights in front of a camera on a tall tripod. The voice resumed:

"Hold that number on the stand next to you in front of your chest and face the camera. Look at the camera. Don't move and don't change your facial expression."

Click. Click.

"Make a half turn to your right and keep your head up."

Click. Click.

"OK, turn to the other side."

Click. Click.

By now, I really felt like a non-person. The fact that I was well dressed and held a graduate degree had no meaning. I was just another Black man in the criminal "just us" system. As directed, I walked up a flight of stairs to an indoor bridge area between the jail and the courthouse.

A well-dressed blond attorney met me in the courtroom.

"Hi, I'm Michael Pelavin," he said as he held out his right hand while holding a bundle of papers in the other. "I've been retained to represent you before the judge here today."

When my case was called, he spoke on my behalf. The judge set bond at $2,000, requiring a deposit of $200 and set a trial date for June 19, 1968. Neither arresting officer showed up at the trial. I was scheduled to start my new position at the University of Iowa June first.

In a letter to the court dated July 17, 1968, Michael Pelavin wrote the following to the court:

"Gentlemen: This office represents Mr. Phillip Jones, a former teacher at Northern

High School. … In June of this year, Mr. Jones was arrested by a city of Flint police officer and charged with interfering with a legal arrest. He was arraigned …bond set in the amount of $200. … The matter was scheduled for trial…on June 19, 1968… Mr. Jones was present in court, ready and able to proceed. The case was adjourned at that time over defense counsel's objection due to the inability of a material witness for the prosecution to be present. At that time, I informed the judge that Mr. Jones was leaving Flint to accept a position at the University of Iowa in Iowa City. The judge was informed that July 10, 1968, was not a workable date for the defense attorney or the principal of Northern High School because they were both going to be out of town. The judge refused to change the date, and, consequently, the $200 bail bond was forfeited."

Pelavin's letter was an appeal to reinstate and return the bond to the bondsman. This was my maiden voyage into the law enforcement and judicial systems. It was shocking to learn firsthand what many undereducated poor people – especially poor Black men – perceive that the penalty phase of the justice system most often means "just us." I experienced the tragedy of self-imposed victimization that so many Black people experience in the name of getting back at "The Man." Being arrested and put in jail for even a short period of time caused me to reflect seriously about the conditions I grew up in and how fortunate I was to have had a loving mother who always had high expectations for my behavior.

My experiences in Flint compelled me to be committed to working with young people to foster and teach self-respect, self-confidence, pride, and taking responsibility for one's actions.

In subsequent correspondence in August and October 1968, after hearing from me, my attorney requested a jury trial set for October 28 or 29, 1968. The trial was never set, the charges were dropped, and the cash bond was returned. In July 1968, Fred Doderer, the director of personnel at the University of Iowa, who was not responsible for the position I had, received an unsigned letter from Flint. The letter contained the newspaper article about my arrest and accusations that I had started the riot. He called me to give me the information and the article. Fred was aware of my experiences in Flint, as was my boss Don Rhodes, the dean of admissions. Both continued to support my efforts at the University.

The anonymous letter from Flint wasn't the only fallout from my arrest. Northern Principal Don Bentley had recommended me to be a paid member of an all-city summer teachers' committee to select new American history textbooks reflecting racial and ethnic diversity. I had received the books for review before the end of the semester. I also had been appointed, based on a recommendation from Francis Bentley, to assist in a summer clinic for high school wrestlers throughout the city. During the week following my arrest, I was dismissed from both positions.

Since I was about to leave town, I could have avoided this terrible experience by simply ignoring the commotion outside the school. However, I believe in standing up for what I believe is right. I adhere to the notion that no one can ride your back if it isn't bent.

Chapter Four:

Starting The EOP

National Scope

Minority recruitment programs redefined student affairs. At the Massachusetts Institute of Technology in 1982, during the first national conference on issues facing Black administrators at predominantly white colleges and universities, former president of North Carolina A&T University Dr. Samuel D. Proctor eloquently stated the case:

"The Black administrator on the white campus is a by-product of the revolution that erupted in the 1960s and that revised the entire landscape of our country. Anyone who was old enough to be aware of the contour of American society before 1960 will remember how different the scene was then from what it is now."

The concept of EOP evolved from a societal need to address a national need to create new ways of providing academic preparation for people historically excluded from broad-based college education. As EOP directors, we were novices in the institutions we were entering and the systems we were innovating.

Many of our initiatives functioned on the periphery of campuses, literally and figuratively. Administratively we were frequently placed in administrative support areas such as student affairs and often located on campuses' outskirts. Many EOP efforts, which came to be known as TRIO programs (Upward Bound, Talent Search and Special Services for disadvantaged students) were totally or significantly supported by federal funds. Program directors had few if any staff for student recruitment or seeing to their students' needs once they were on campus. We used explicit proposals and implicit improvisation to modify or create institutional programs and services to support our students.

We were responsible to administrators who knew less about developing a new concept of educational opportunity than we knew. Despite insufficient financial resources, we started with great enthusiasm and passion to expand opportunities for a college education for historically excluded students.

Orientation

Emphasis on expanding diversity was the basis of an exchange program initiated in 1965 by the University of Iowa under President Howard Bowen with historically black Rust College in Holly Springs, Mississippi, and Le Moyne-Owen College in Memphis, Tennessee. President Bowen extended the University's commitment to human rights by creating the Martin Luther King (MLK) Scholarship Program in 1968.

I believe Donald "Dusty" Rhodes, dean of admissions and records, recruited me for the position of admissions coordinator at the University of Iowa because I lived the experiences of students I recruited. My indigenous expertise was my greatest asset for this position.

Suspicion about the militancy of equal-opportunity program (EOP) directors was a common concern. My position was highly publicized before I was hired. President Bowen announced the creation of the MLK program four days after King's assassination and subsequent Black rebellions in cities across the country. I was recruited, interviewed, and hired within eight weeks after the announcement. I had a public profile from the beginning.

I was invited to speak at practically every service club breakfast or lunch in town. I sensed some wanted to hear my thoughts about civil rights, to gauge my militancy, or to learn if I was so strident that I would upset the community. EOP directors were publicly evaluated in the local, regional, and national press. A writer profiled me in the Sunday magazine of the Des Moines Register, the largest newspaper in the state, and an article announcing my appointment ran in Chicago's Black community newspaper The Chicago Defender. I was careful never to believe my press clippings.

On my first day my new boss, Don, as he asked me to call him, handed me a legal pad and called his administrative assistant Marian Hansen (who became an assistant registrar) who brought into the office with her a young woman named Mary Jane Carlson. She was to be my first secretary. Dean Rhodes then took Mary Jane and me to the third floor of Jessup Hall to our new offices in the corridor between the geography and urban and regional planning offices.

Don and I sat down in my new digs, and he gave me instructions. He told me one of his other employees, Bob Sauers, would work with me to develop a recruiting schedule. Bob was an assistant director of admissions and had been director of admissions at Grinnell College before coming to the University of Iowa.

Don told me he'd asked John Moore, director of financial aid, to work with me as well. John and Bob were invaluable mentors orienting me to the higher education's administrative practices.

Federal grant programs for low income students were in their infancy. Initially, the plan was to rely on private donations to fund the MLK scholarships. Patty Murray, wife of political science professor James Murray, led an effort to raise community funds to initiate the program. Contributions didn't materialize sufficiently, so an alternate plan was developed based on University grant support in conjunction with federal grants and loans. Family contributions were considered when available, and self-help by student recipients was factored into the award formula.

We developed a formula for awarding student aid starting with federal grant criteria followed by federal loans, work/study and parental contributions to fill financial aid packages. Funds from local contributions were marked for students' emergency needs.

Low income students who qualified for full federal support were priority with students having the next levels of greatest need second in line, and before students with little or no financial need being the third priority. The basic program targeted students from educationally and economically disadvantaged backgrounds. Initial emphasis was on Black students but expanded to all students of color as well as white students who fit the definition. The first group of 42 EOP students in 1968 was multiracial. I felt good about the commitment I could then offer incoming students.

The first class of EOP students had been admitted before I came to campus. I had no idea who they were or if they would enroll. I had mixed feelings about the incoming class. What if they didn't come? Would there be housing for all of them? What would students expect the University to do about personal expenses they hadn't anticipated? I was uncomfortable about the situation. I didn't want to have confusion among students that might cause a protest before they were oriented to the campus. Because I had had no communication with the students, I decided to visit some communities in Iowa to learn what I could about the Iowa students' expectations and their communities. I went to Des Moines, Cedar Rapids, Waterloo and Davenport to find the newly admitted EOP students, introduce myself to them and get a sense of their concerns.

I was fascinated by what I learned. Except for those from Waterloo, whose environment and attitude closely mirrored my own, urban Black students in Iowa had different perspectives about relating to white students than what I'd experienced growing up and going to high school and college and teaching in Flint. Most Black students from Iowa's urban areas spoke with the same midwestern dialect as their white peers, but with a rhythm and vernacular like Blacks in urban communities throughout the nation. (We now call this "code-switching," but at that time we didn't have language to describe that fluidity between accents and vocabularies.)

These Black students seemed to move with confidence and closer social distance between themselves and whites than I'd ever witnessed.

Before the MLK scholarship program, targeted recruitment at the University of Iowa was limited to athletes. Bob Sauers and I designed a four-step recruiting program to identify, educate, cultivate, and enroll students. We based the number of new EOP students each year on the amount of University support available to supplement federal grant and loan funds.

The program's goal was to increase minority populations on campus from within the state of Iowa, which had a nonwhite population of less than 3 percent, urban areas in neighboring states as well as southern states from where many students of color had come in the past. We didn't ignore other parts of the country, especially when alumni brought students to our attention. Our recruiting goals were for seventy percent non-resident and thirty percent resident minority students. I was proud of praise I heard from community talent search and high school counselors for the clarity of University commitments to recruits from their communities.

The University of Iowa's initial efforts were unique in comparison to other Big Ten and large public research universities in 1967. States with larger nonwhite populations tended to concentrate only on in-state students. Iowa also appropriated money to support student financial aid, recruiting, and EOP administration before federal dollars became the norm for funding disadvantaged student programs.

Law College Initiatives

Initial efforts to admit African American students began with the College of Law. The first Black graduate, Alexander Clark, received his Bachelor of Law degree in 1879. Yet in 1967, there were no Black students in the law school. So, Dean David Vernon, appointed just a year earlier, initiated one of the first Council on Legal Education Opportunity (CLEO) programs to increase Black lawyers in the country. The first student admitted under the new initiative in 1966 was an outstanding college basketball player from Southern Illinois University named Eddie Blythe. Aggressive recruiting led by Paul Neuhauser, associate dean of the college, led to four Black students enrolling in 1967, a similar number in 1968 and twelve minority students in 1969.

The College of Law's commitment was an effort that included a concerted push to recruit outstanding minority faculty during the same period. George Strait, a Black law professor who was associate law librarian at Harvard University, became the head of the University of Iowa Law Library in 1976 and was a tireless recruiter of Black faculty and students until his retirement in 1985. By the fall of 1995, more than twenty percent of students in the law school were people of color and about thirteen percent of the faculty was non-white.

Standardized admissions exams with their implicit cultural biases were the object of great criticism from Black educators like Dr. William "Bill" Parker an administrator with the Educational Testing Service that produced the law school admissions test, also known as the LSAT. Bill looked more like an NFL tight end than an expert on tests and measurements. A native of Cairo, Illinois, he experienced southern-style segregation and discrimination in education. Bill was a devoted advocate for helping minority students master standardized tests.

In the mid-1970s, during a casual conversation at a national meeting, I mentioned to Bill and Silas Purnell – who had a great track record of placing Black students in law schools – a program I was working on for a grant I'd received from the U.S. Office (now Department) of Education for training EOP directors in higher education administration. We were discussing how best to prepare Black students to be more successful on admissions tests.

"I have an idea about a program to give students a preparatory experience for the LSAT," Bill said. "We would provide sample questions that could be administered to students the year before they take the test. We'd give the students some basic background about test preparation and test taking skills, but most importantly they could learn what law school is all about. All we need is a law school to agree to underwrite the program. I could provide all the testing materials they'd need, and we could help them set it up and run it. Then they could take it over and run it every year."

Bill and Silas knew what other universities were doing to expand opportunities in law schools and other programs, so I was impressed by their faith in the University of Iowa for initiating this program.

"Iowa is the ideal place to start," Silas quickly followed. "They have a definite commitment to minority students, and I think the dean would be open to the idea."

In the 1970s, Dean N. William "Bill" Hines became dean of the University of Iowa College of Law. Bill, an easygoing, straight-talking, affable advocate for human rights, who loved to play pick-up basketball, met with Bill Parker and Si Purnell to discuss the proposal. He was impressed and advocated the program with the law school faculty, who agreed to host the program. Bill Hines, Bill Parker, and Si Purnell conferred, planned, and established the Iowa Bridging the Gap Minority Pre-Law Conference in 1978, which became an annual event hosted at the University of Iowa College of Law for minority law school aspirants throughout the nation.

Medical College

Colleges of medicine didn't have student support programs prior to the invention of EOP. At its annual meeting in 1968, the American Association of Medical Colleges (AAMC) endorsed the concept that minority representation in medical schools should be increased. Financial aid wasn't a standard administrative entity in colleges of medicine before the creation of disadvantaged student initiatives. National Medical Fellowships, a nonprofit organization, increased the amount of scholarship aid to minority students. The Robert Wood Johnson Foundation provided money to U.S. medical schools as scholarships for minority students.

In the 1960s the federal government created financial aid programs known as the Health Professions Loans and Health Professions Scholarships to help support health sciences students. These programs were significant factors in increasing the numbers of low-income people in the health professions and important for assisting EOP students in medicine, dentistry, pharmacy, and nursing programs at Iowa.

When I started in EOP, the University of Iowa's College of Medicine was just beginning to implement such programs. The only student services counseling available in the college was from Dr. Woodrow "Woody" Morris, a psychologist in the dean's office. Woody assisted students with personal and financial issues. I met with him to establish a support system for EOP medical students.

University of Iowa College of Medicine Dean Robert Hardin and his successor Jack Eckstein initiated recruitment of minority students for the college in 1968. Hardin invited me to a faculty meeting held in the semicircular, steeply tiered theater in the old medical research building. The rows of white coats gave me the impression of white faces among clouds rising to the top of the room.

I stood at the base of the amphitheater looking up into the ivory sea as Hardin introduced the topic of the meeting. I began by explaining the EOP's structure. I then described the personal qualities of people I knew who aspired to study medicine and how so many of them had the desire and tenacity to persevere but not necessarily the test scores or finances to pursue their dreams. I outlined intangible qualities I sought to identify minority candidates with the academic potential and personal maturity to overcome disadvantaged backgrounds and achieve their goal to become doctors.

When I invited questions, a physician about halfway up the rows stood and began to talk about you people. I listened patiently to his reservations about the perceived shortcomings of you people – of course meaning "Black people." I experienced an immediate rush in my chest and urge to attack his comments, but I remained calm and silent as he spoke. I felt that the best way to refute his remarks was to address the social connotation of the term he used to characterize Black people. I said,

"The term you people implicitly infers inferior status to Black people. The subtle prejudice expressed in such a comment may reinforce perceptions that negate any chance for equality of opportunity in education or employment of otherwise qualified people."

Other faculty members spoke in support of what at least one saw as the college's moral obligation to help the disadvantaged. A unanimous vote followed to begin the College of Medicine's EOP later that year. The college admitted William Anderson, a PhD degree candidate in pharmacy, as the first EOP medical student in September 1968.

Don Rhodes chaired the admissions committee as well as a newly formed EOP medical admissions subcommittee that reviewed minority applicants and forwarded the most promising ones to the full admissions committee. I provided background information to the subcommittee about outstanding personal attributes I identified in each individual applicant. The EOP faculty committee paid close attention to issues related to maintaining excellence in academic performance and standards while expanding the diversity of the student body.

The program's goal was to admit minority students based on an expanded set of criteria while expecting them to achieve academic success as effectively as their non-EOP counterparts. The program's structure allowed students to begin in the summer to facilitate entry and academic progress. To lighten the load of the difficult first semester, students were required to complete one course for credit and an in-depth overview of two other subject areas during the summer and therefore only had two credit courses in their first semester.

The program developed a wide range of support services to orient students to systematic ways to learn large amounts of cognitively complex material that characterized subjects in an ever-expanding medical curriculum. As students progressed, the services evolved into the coordination of four years of supportive activity rather than a pre-entry or first-year support program which laid the groundwork for an all-college Office of the Associate Dean for Student Affairs and Curriculum. Professor George Baker, a pediatrician, was the office's first administrator. His duties expanded from overseeing the supportive services for the EOP to administering the office for the entire college.

By this time, the EOP admissions process was entirely under the College of Medicine. Under Dr. Baker, the college received a national grant to establish a learning center. The basic premise was to enhance students' learning efficiency for the vast cognitive complexity in medical education and training programs.

The center's initial purpose focused on EOP students. Rosalyn Beecham (Green)

– one of the first EOP undergraduates – was appointed to coordinate the early program. The learning center's scope broadened to include all medical students. Student support services – including admissions and financial aid – are now regular administrative areas in most if not all colleges of medicine in the U.S.

Evolving Policies

Retention and placement were not priorities in research public universities before the emphasis on recruiting minority students. University officials assumed that, to be successful, disadvantaged students needed special attention in academic advising, financial support, tutoring, and counseling – services seen as necessities to retain disadvantaged students but of little value or import to privileged students.

The EOP at Iowa preceded appointment of professional academic advisers to supplement faculty advisers for the general student body. Positive outcomes of opportunity programs for disadvantaged students demonstrated the value of support services for the retention and success for all students.

Summer orientation, now a staple for all new students, was initiated at Iowa to give EOP students a head start to acclimate them to their new environment. Our first summer pre-registration at the University happened in 1968 for the first group of EOP students. Students arrived for a week before beginning the fall semester for academic advising, placement screening, and to become familiar with the campus and community. Today, every incoming class starts with summer orientation.

Iowa's first career fair, another event now open to all learners, was first organized for EOP students in 1972.

Health History Inclusion

When universities began systematic recruitment of educationally and economically disadvantaged students, it was a given that financial aid was the greatest barrier to overcome in supporting students. Consideration of physical and mental health and wellness issues weren't part of the equation. Soon after EOP students arrived on campuses, directors began to hear complaints from students about their eyes, teeth, hearing, and breathing.

Some students had never had what we would consider routine medical or dental checkups. Except for participation in high school athletics, the first physical examination some students received as teenagers was required for admission to the university. As a result, some of our students had undiagnosed illnesses or chronic health problems.

Impoverished communities often lack adequate health facilities, just as many low-income families often have inadequate health insurance if they have any coverage at all. Many students persist despite health issues.

At the beginning of EOP we had given some thought to possible needs for emergency dollars, and the MLK fund became the designated source covering costs of unforeseen health issues.

Initially, I didn't recognize the importance of health and wellness in educating the whole person. These lessons were the basis for initiatives I took to develop fitness centers in residence halls, lounges in the Iowa Memorial Union, and a campus recreation/wellness center when I became dean of students and vice president for student services.

As time passed, health and wellness have become central areas of student development for all learners. Mandatory student health insurance, therapeutic recreation, and wellness programs have replaced the once-required physical education courses at many colleges and universities.

Community Inclusion

In 1968, there were fewer than one hundred fifty Black students on campus and less than half were undergraduate women. Recruiting undergraduate students, other than athletes, was practically nonexistent at public research universities before race- and economic-based equal opportunity programs began. Recruiting students of color to attend the University of Iowa was, and still is, a matter of personal contact. I learned early in my career that to get the best outcomes, I used the same approach coaches used to attract the best students for athletic team participation.

I got to know the students, their families, and their communities to counteract negative stereotypes about predominantly white universities in general and the University of Iowa specifically. I felt the apprehension keenly whenever I met with a group of students. I approached speaking to them as though they were feeling as I did when I transferred to the University of Illinois in Champaign-Urbana. I sensed the tightness in the belly and reluctance to speak they may have felt. My challenge was to help them learn, as I had, to feel comfortable and secure in a new cultural environment.

My first recruiting plan in Iowa was designed to visit high schools with low-income and minority students in western and eastern border cities. The schedule spanned three states and was taxing but enlightening. I spent every other week on the road visiting schools and communities from Omaha to Des Moines to Moline and throughout the area. I visited more than thirty-five high schools to learn if they had viable recruiting populations and to introduce the University of Iowa's plan to expand equality of opportunity to these students and their peers.

It was not unusual to enter a school and hear the counselors explain cordially that their buildings didn't have students who qualified for such a program. On several occasions, I experienced delicate interpersonal situations because school staff members were uncomfortable and embarrassed about discussing racial issues.

In one high school, in a small Iowa town outside Des Moines, I met with two white female counselors who were eagerly awaiting my prearranged visit. Their faces dropped when I walked into the room. They looked at each other and warmly – but uncomfortably – welcomed me and shook my hand. As we stumbled through introductory small talk, one of the women smiled broadly, and in a soothingly condescending voice, looked straight at me and said, "How did you get that job?" Ignoring my immediate recognition of her unintentional micro-aggression, I took her question at face value.

"I was recruited from a teaching position in Michigan to return to the University of Iowa – where I received my master's degree – to work to expand human rights," I replied. The women both seemed pleased and genuinely hospitable after I recited my truncated résumé.

Each city had a different character, and the attitudes of Black students varied between towns. I was somewhat familiar with the students in Cedar Rapids and Davenport, each city within an hour's drive of Iowa City, because I had worked with many of them in the Upward Bound Program the summer before I graduated from the University of Iowa in 1967. The Cedar Rapids students were generally comfortable in their surroundings but not especially ambitious about going to college. Most Black students in Cedar Rapids attended Washington High School. I had a difficult time getting their attention to be serious about going to college. It was as though they had been integrated into oblivion. They seemed to be content with their less than adequate economic and social situations.

Davenport, a city on the western bank of the Mississippi River, had a mixture of Iowa and Illinois flavor. Many adults worked in industry for John Decre or the Alcoa manufacturing company while others worked in federal employment for the Rock Island Arsenal in Illinois. Black students seemed to have a clear identity and Latino students seemed to live in a close-knit community. There was a clear but not contentious racial separation in Davenport. Many students indicated a need to be ambitious.

Neighboring Rock Island, on the other hand, seemed like a different world for Black people. The students I talked to at Rock Island High School were difficult to reach. Many didn't comprehend that new opportunities were available to them. Moline, another nearby Quad City, was a different story. The few Black students there shared their Latino counterparts' middle-class aspirations.

Waterloo, a little more than eighty miles north of Iowa City, reminded me of neighborhoods in Chicago that housed participants in the Great Migration. Waterloo's predominately Black east side had a southern flair. From the 1920s until it closed in 1985, the Rath Packing Company. was a major employer of Black southerners who traveled on the Illinois Central Railroad to Waterloo, the end of the rail line.

The east side of Waterloo, like Chicago's south and west sides, is basically a segregated Black community. Black students, though not a majority, were a plurality at Waterloo East High School. They were among the most exciting young people I met on my first sojourn through the state. I found great support there for students in a white senior counselor named John Lowe and his wife. Black residents such as Mrs. Anna Mae Weems – a community activist who sent two daughters and a son to the University of Iowa for undergraduate study and law school – offered the same. I conducted many recruiting visits at the home of Weems and her husband Vernon.

I went to Tama-Toledo High School in Tama, located seventy-one miles northwest of Iowa City, to recruit Native American students from the Meskwaki Settlement. The Settlement had its own primary school, but the teens attended high school in Tama-Toledo. A broad, middle-aged man with thinning blond hair greeted me at the high school with a wide smile and boundless enthusiasm. It was probably obvious who I was, given that there didn't seem to be other Black people in the town, or at least I hadn't seen any as I drove to the school.

We walked a short distance down a corridor flanked by neat student lockers to a brightly painted nicely furnished conference room. He opened the door and motioned for me to enter ahead of him. Two smiling women, one with a stylish blond hairdo, and the other brunette with gray streaks in her hair, rose from their chairs as I approached the conference table. Though they were smiling and acting polite I had the uncomfortable feeling that the native students were not their primary concern.

"Welcome to Tama-Toledo High School," one woman said. "We thought Iowa would be coming in the first week in October to talk to our juniors about applying for admission to Iowa for next year. Did we misunderstand your schedule?"

"I'm the new admissions coordinator in the Office of Admissions to expand educational opportunities for minority and low-income students," I explained, still standing. "I received a confirmation to meet today with Native American students. You're correct about the date for admissions information for the junior class; that will be the first week in October."

The counselors looked at one another sheepishly.

"There must have been a misunderstanding," the gentleman began to offer an explanation.

"That's not a problem, and we can assemble the students without any difficulty in just a few minutes," the tall brunette lady interrupted.

She rose to leave the room. Moments later a bell rang to change classes, and the counselor's voice came over the intercom speakers.

"Would Indian students please come to the counselors' conference room? Thank you," she said.

I was stunned, but I tried to stay cool. My viscera tightened, and I sensed a churning sensation. I was upset about what seemed to be an insensitive public announcement. I felt no animus toward the counselors because they expressed the same genuine hospitality I sensed from the white female counselors outside Des Moines who needed to hear my credentials.

The counselors in Tama seemed oblivious to the negative social connotation of their tone and phrasing. I sensed an act of unconcern for the feelings of a small disadvantaged population of students with distinct cultural mores being singled out in a predominantly white environment away from the comfort zone of their own community.

I waited in the conference room after the three counselors excused themselves. They seemed to want to respect the privacy of my conversation with the students. I wondered why they weren't curious to learn what I would say and how they might be of assistance to the students in applying for college. They never said whether the Native American students were included in the junior class college recruitment meeting with the University of Iowa admissions office. I sensed that my conference with them became unimportant once they realized I wasn't the regular University of Iowa representative.

No students came in during the first period class. Later two young men and one young woman opened the door and looked in inquisitively.

"Is this where we're supposed to be?" asked the first male student. I tried to be upbeat because I didn't have a feeling of positive energy from any of them when they saw me. I felt a little embarrassed about being the person they'd meet without any warning, not knowing how they might react to a Black person when they may not have ever interacted with one before. We met briefly. They were very polite and silent. After I made a few short remarks, I thought it prudent to thank them for coming and, then, to try to find another way to reach Native American students outside of the school.

I had worked with students from the Meskwaki Settlement in the Upward Bound Program. One – a bright, quiet and artistic student named Ruth Pushetonequa – was among the forty-two first year EOP students. Ruth is the granddaughter of an elder of the Settlement's Bear clan. I talked to her about my visit. She listened quietly.

"That's not the way you approach kids from the Settlement," she said in a somber, matter-of-fact manner. "You need to talk to my grandfather, George Young Bear, to get the word to their parents. If you want me to, I'll talk to my grandfather about what you want to do, and I could go with you to the Settlement to meet with him." We met with Ruth's grandfather, and established a link for future contacts on the Settlement.

Faculty Support

For many members of the University of Iowa's faculty, creating EOP was a transforming experience. As the program developed, many efforts by faculty went beyond the classroom and lecture halls on students' behalf. It became apparent to me that social change was a priority for faculty I worked with. Professor of History David Schoenbaum followed several students beyond their years as his advisees or in his classes. He routinely made a point of informing me, even after I was no longer EOP director, about bright students of color in his classes who might be underperforming due to cultural differences. Lane Davis, a professor in political science, was another person who went out of his way to help nonwhite students adjust to the community academically and socially.

At national meetings, Professors Dee Norton and Milt Rosenbaum both in the Department of Psychology made it their business to identify Black graduate students whom they felt could be successful in their highly competitive graduate programs. The psychology department's assessment of nonwhite candidates' potential went beyond the standard scores on the Graduate Record Examination (GRE) exam.

Professor Richard "Dick" Braddock and Professor Louise "Lou" Kelley in the Department of English and Rhetoric recommended, planned, and administered writing exercises for the first group of EOP students. During their summers, Dick and Lou met with the students, conducted, and reviewed the writings, and then recommended students for either the preparatory, regular, or advanced first year rhetoric classes. Most of the students didn't lack writing skills. In fact, some placed in the advanced rhetoric class.

With this experience it became clear to many faculty and administrators that while EOP students came from educationally and economically disadvantaged backgrounds that prevented access to exemplary education, they were not culturally deprived or intellectually deficient and did not need lowered standards. Their life experiences are affected by residential red-lining, housing discrimination, unemployment, low wages, job discrimination, underfunded, ill-equipped, inadequately staffed schools, and low social expectations that mitigate against, what sociologist Max Weber called, increasing life chances for economic and social mobility.

The students were expected to complete regular courses and make reasonable progress toward completing their degree programs – just like their privileged peers. The EOP provided voluntary tutoring and advising both to students with academic needs as well as to those who wanted extra help to excel in their classes. The program's basic philosophy was that students were responsible for their own behavior. However, I had an active, and intrusive, approach to encourage them to be productive.

The Students

When I started at Iowa, I learned quickly that many in the community perceived positions like mine as an opportunity Black people had never had. African Americans tended to cluster in professions characterized as teaching, preaching and social work. EOP directors created opportunities to be conduits of verbal assessments for unrecognized drive, motivation and intelligence for their institutions that outside the Black community had not previously been taken seriously.

Students from backgrounds as mine lacked then, and still do, the educational and cultural experiences to improve their life chances in ways comparable to traditional entering students in predominantly white institutions. When we started recruiting nonwhite and economically disadvantaged students, we sought to provide economic and educational support for them to excel in highly competitive academic programs at research universities. I believe students will succeed if motivated to minimize their educational disadvantages. My approach was to treat students as individuals and educate each whole person.

Jo and I moved into university housing at the beginning of our tenure in Iowa City with financial resources at about the same level as our graduate student neighbors. We were living in one of the Hawkeye Court – now demolished – complex two-bedroom apartments with our seven-month-old daughter Phyllis. On a hot and humid Sunday afternoon in mid-August, while she and I played on the floor, the phone rang.

"Hello? Yes, this is Phillip Jones' house," I heard Jo say. "Yes, he is. Just one moment please."

She turned to me.

"This is for you. It's one of your new students at the bus station." Jo handed me the phone.

"Hello Mr. Jones, this is Hope Carter from Cuthbert, Georgia," said the voice on the other end. "I just got into Iowa City. I'm at the bus station. Can you tell me where I'm supposed to go?"

Cuthbert is a town of about three thousand people in the southwest corner of Georgia. It is about seventy-five percent Black, and most residents are low income. Cuthbert's claims to fame is being the hometown of the great jazz pianist and orchestra leader, Fletcher Henderson, and Larry Holmes, former heavyweight boxing champion.

Hope was an outstanding high school student. A local white Iowa alum who read about EOP in an alumni publication encouraged Hope to apply to the University of Iowa. He'd never traveled far from his hometown, let alone left Georgia.

It was the weekend before students were to arrive on campus for the pre-semester workshop and orientation to campus life – Iowa's first ever for freshmen.

The phone call from Hope was my first contact with a new out-of-state student. Immediately, I wondered what I should do to get him settled into the residence hall. He obviously had no means of transportation for himself and his belongings. We had bought a used car just before we left Flint. Jo's father found a used 1962 Chevrolet station wagon that I bought for six hundred dollars. I had gone to Decatur, Illinois, to pick up the car and drive it back to Flint. It came in handy to move Hope's trunk, two suitcases and typewriter.

There weren't many people on campus. I recalled my early days in Champaign and the feeling of being left alone for the first time in a strange place. I thought it might be more intense for someone so far away from home in a place so different and with no family connections to depend on.

I decided Jo, Phyllis, and I would be his family for his first day on campus. Meager as it was, Hawkeye Court would have to be our hosting place.

"I'm going down to the bus station to pick up this student, and bring him home to have dinner with us, if that's all right with you?" I said to Jo.

"If you want to bring him into this little hotbox with baby stuff all over the floor, its fine with me," she laughed.

When I arrived at the bus station, which was a converted gas station in downtown Iowa City, I noticed a broad shouldered muscular young man with slight facial hair and a medium-length Afro. He was standing unassumingly next to his belongings in the shade of the building. Since we were the only two Black people in the vicinity, it seemed reasonable that we would recognize each other.

"You must be Hope," I said rhetorically.

"Yes, sir," he replied in a low-key way that I now recognize as characteristic of the understated manner he displayed throughout his undergraduate career. Hope had a natural cool and quiet self-confidence that allowed him to reveal his lack of sophistication when he frequently asked naïve questions. Hope was open about saying where he was from, and he made coming from a small Georgia town the basis for getting people to teach him about where they were from. The way Hope absorbed things about his new environment and his questions about people, places, and things, clearly indicated he was outside his personal comfort zone, but nevertheless anxious to learn as much as he could as soon as he could.

"You've had a long trip, and you must be tired and hot. If you'd like, you can come home with me to get something to eat and relax a little bit before we get you checked into the dorm. Our place is small, but we'll try to make you comfortable," I said.

"Yes sir, that would be great," he said with an easy smile as his expression brightened and his shoulders relaxed.

Hope was polite to Jo and me, and very much at ease with baby Phyllis. He symbolized what EOP would mean in creating innovative approaches to respond to the backgrounds and needs of students of color.

Early Monday morning before the first EOP summer workshop and orientation, a tall striking young man with sepia-toned skin accented by his metal-rimmed eyeglasses and gold capped front teeth came into my office wearing a serious-but-pleasant facial expression.

"How ya doin this morning?"

"I'm Percy Watson, and I've got some questions about the limit you've got on taking less than a full load of classes at twelve semester hours of credit instead of fifteen or seventeen hours of credit each semester. I don't want to be limited to less than a full load because I intend to get my degree in three years, so I can go to law school and get finished in two years," he spoke confidently.

"That's a great goal, Percy," I replied, "but twelve hours isn't a requirement. We've done that to ensure that EOP students can receive institutional financial aid for ten semesters if they need to reduce their academic loads to complete their degrees." I paused to catch my breath. "You're not required to limit your registration to twelve hours. I think it will be great if you earned your degree in three years."

"Well, that's what I intend to do," he said.

And so, began my introduction to Percy, a young man from a historically segregated school system in Hattiesburg, Mississippi – one of the Civil Rights Movement's landmark cities. There, Percy graduated first in his high-school class, yet had an ACT composite score that ranked in the lowest 10 percent of his freshman class at the University of Iowa.

In Iowa City, Percy was a highly active undergraduate committed to social change and Black chauvinism. Metaphorically, Percy was so Black that he wouldn't eat white rice. He organized a group to promote what he called "the Black Law," which emphasized Black pride in the academic and social principles he devised.

Percy was very comfortable in interactions on both sides of the veil. He participated in campus activities and encouraged his Black Law comrades to achieve academic excellence. He was always polite and displayed southern charm in addressing his elders as "ma'am" and "sir."

Percy, like other Black college students attending predominantly white institutions in the mid- to late 1960s, engaged vocally in what I call "Black-over-rap." These students spouted strident rhetoric while participating in the university's bureaucracy.

He and other Black students reminded me of how my peers and I felt in the early 1960s. We wanted to find ways to be relevant in the struggle even though we were not in the South. So, we engaged in symbolic protests by picketing chain stores in Chicago to protest segregated lunch counters in the South.

The campus militants of the late 1960s had similar feelings about being relevant to the urban struggles for equal rights in the North. They were also encouraged to emulate the militancy of Black campus demonstrations, making demands of campus administrators, and shutting down campuses when their demands were ignored.

At Iowa, Black students demanded relevance in the curriculum and inclusion in campus life and in university culture. The BSU gathered at the Afro American Cultural Center – also known as the Afro House – to caucus about their concerns.

"There's no recognition of Black people on this campus," Percy said one night. "I've been to the library to look up the history of Black folk at Iowa, and I found that there are a lot a Black people who are important in the history of this place."

He briefed everyone on Archie A. Alexander, the first Black person to graduate in engineering at Iowa, who designed Iowa City's Burlington Street bridge which students use to cross the Iowa River and travel between the east and west campuses and Elizabeth Catlett, a Black woman who earned the University's first Master of Fine Arts degree.

Percy concluded his sermon by urging the audience to demand the administration rename Iowa Stadium in honor of Duke Slater, the Iowa Hawkeyes football team's first Black All-American – who later used the law degree he earned from Iowa to become a municipal court judge in Chicago.

BSU members then wrote a proposal to President Willard "Sandy" Boyd, who arranged a meeting to discuss the students' request with me, Vice President Philip G. Hubbard, and Iowa College of Law Dean David Vernon. Sandy never ignored demands from activists – Black or white. He always considered the human rights implications of students' concerns and brought them up with his vice presidents – and frequently with me. He and his administration always had a reasoned and humanistic approach that recognized the university as a serious forum for the free exchange of ideas and regarded demands from the disenfranchised – even when those demands conflicted with what Boyd and his cabinet thought was best.

Sandy, Phil, and David also were politically astute. They felt the BSU's proposal had merit but might alienate many fans and alumni who believed other football All Americans were equally or worthier of such recognition. No Division I football stadiums were named after Black individuals at the time, and Iowa wasn't ready to make history. We decided to name the stadium after Nile Kinnick, a football icon at Iowa and the only Heisman trophy winner in the team's history. Kinnick was also an outstanding student and World War II hero who died during his service. In a poignant twist for Iowa fans, the distinction of having the first and only Division I football stadium named after a Black person went to Iowa State University's Jack Trice Stadium – home of the Hawkeyes' in-state rival.

In 1966 and 1968, twin high-rise residence halls opened on Grand Avenue west of the Iowa River adjacent to the athletic field house and the health sciences campus. The buildings were named in recognition of a former dean of the College of Medicine.

After much discussion, Sandy and Phil decided that it would be a more appropriate symbol to rename one of the two high-rise residence halls – originally named for former Iowa College of Medicine Dean Robert E. Rienow – after Slater. Their rationale was that having a residence hall be the first campus building to bear the name of a Black individual would emphasize progress in human rights, because Slater, like all of the University's Black students, was prohibited from living in campus residence. This policy was overturned in 1946-1947. In 2016, the University of Iowa proposed to the Property and Facilities Committee of the Board of Regents, State of Iowa, to name a new residence hall in recognition of a female Black student who changed history. The board approved, and Elizabeth Catlett Residence Hall opened in fall 2017.

Percy earned his degree in political science in three years and was elected to Phi Beta Kappa, the first EOP student recognized for such an academic honor. He graduated from the University of Iowa College of Law in two and a half years. The avowed Black chauvinist and committed southerner then took a position with a firm in Alaska. After a short time, he returned to Hattiesburg with his wife – whom he met at Iowa – and family to practice law. Voters elected Percy to the Mississippi Legislature in 1980.

Percy was the first of many EOP students to help spur substantial change on the Iowa campus and the city surrounding it. Mae Colleen Thompson, a young woman from Kansas City, Missouri, who was always upbeat, bright, and in charge of every situation she was involved in, was another. One of the "Kansas City Nine" that assistant basketball coach Lanny Van Eman recruited, Colleen – as she preferred people call her – was in my office almost daily. Colleen was a student in the College of Liberal Arts and intended to enter the College of Business after her first year.

She had an outstanding record at the historically Black Central High School, but her ACT composite was below average in comparison to her freshman class at Iowa. Colleen's personality neutralized the dual consciousness effects of the racial veil; she had no difficulty relating to students from all different backgrounds, but she also was an intellectual militant when it came to Black pride and equal opportunities.

Because she was a regular in my office, we discussed ideas about how to make the campus community more livable for Black students. We talked about planning a recognition program in February for Black History Month. I told her how I had initiated something similar in 1968 at Northern High School in Flint. She was excited by the idea, so I put her in charge of organizing the program as part of EOP. She created the first program's theme, "Perspectives: Black on Black."

Maceo Mitchell, a Black graduate student in the School of Art and Art History's MFA degree program, provided one of his intaglio prints to create a poster advertising the event. I was visiting Omaha North High School in Nebraska when I decided to go to the barber shop of Ernest "Ernie" Chambers, the only Black member of the state's legislature. Chambers was an outspoken civil rights advocate who received national recognition for his efforts in Nebraska. He agreed to be the keynote speaker for our first Black History Month celebration.

For a class project, Colleen and fellow student Kathy Duchen created an on-campus experience for disadvantaged Black elementary school children from Waterloo to encourage them to aspire toward going to college and to familiarize them with that environment. Kathy was a confident white student, open minded, and secure in her attitudes about race and poverty. She demonstrated a practical sense of caring that personified the essence of her degree program in the College of Nursing. Colleen and Kathy named their class project "Keyhole: Opening Doors to Opportunity."

The pair solicited funds and support from local merchants, student government, and University departments and colleges. The EOP paid for buses, meals and materials for the children, teachers, and chaperones. The program consisted of a tour of the hospital, where the children had their blood pressures taken and their eyes examined; a tour of the dental college, where they had brief dental exams and received toothbrushes and small tubes of toothpaste; a tour of the basketball court at the Field House, and lunch in one of the residence halls.

Kathy's father, former president of the Younkers department stores Charles Duchen, donated two thousand dollars as seed money to continue the Keyhole project. It led to a succession of similar initiatives, including a partnership between EOP, Lincoln Elementary School in Waterloo, and UI College of Education faculty to improve student reading skills.

Keyhole and EOP established ongoing pen pal programs and campus visits for elementary children of color in Cedar Rapids and West Branch, as well as an initiative to bring Black high school jazz musicians to perform at the Iowa City Jazz Festival. With support from the Roy J. Carver disadvantaged student fund, the hope was that the students, all from urban areas, would interact with Iowa counterparts to foster diversity and understanding. Keyhole programs continued after Colleen and Kathy graduated.

In addition to her activism, Colleen was an outstanding student. She was one of a very small number of Black students in the College of Business and was inducted into the academic honorary Mortar Board Society. After Iowa, she earned an MBA degree from the University of Southern California and a doctorate in business from George Washington University. She met and married a student from Memphis in the first EOP class. Melvin Jones, an introspective student with a quiet assertive streak for competition and confrontation for social change, interned in the Internal Revenue Service in Cedar Rapids and went on to become the vice president for business and administration at the historically Black Howard University. Before his untimely death in his mid-fifties, Melvin was vice president for finance at the University of Nebraska while Colleen worked as a professor in the school's College of Business Administration.

Despite students' successes and positive influence beyond Iowa City, EOP's value wasn't accepted universally. Detractors believed Black students took places that belonged to their more qualified white peers. These beliefs caused me great anxiety. I saw my job as motivating students to do their best despite difficult times. That meant earning the students' trust and helping them get started on campus. No matter how much they relied on me, they had to face the pain of adjustment to and learning in a challenging environment. Some students wouldn't make it, and they would need to go somewhere else to finish college. I could help them with many things, but only they could persevere. Some didn't. Many did and still do.

The first wave of EOP students across the country set expectations. At Iowa, academic deans had great interest in making sure these learners maintained high academic standards. Dewey B. Stuit, dean of Iowa's College of Liberal Arts, and his Associate Dean, Hugh Kelso, met periodically with me and Dean of Admissions Don Rhodes during the first semester of my first recruiting year to assess potential EOP students' academic records.

At one of those meetings, I introduced the record of Cornelius "Perk" Thornton, a twenty-seven-year-old Army veteran and college dropout. He and I finished high school together in 1959, and we both spent a year in pre-pharmacy at the University of Illinois in Chicago. Perk left Navy Pier without officially withdrawing.

In the meeting, I made the case for him highlighting his three years of service in an Army Airborne unit stationed in Germany as well as how he was juggling work as a night custodian for the Chicago Public Schools while taking classes during the day at a community college. I knew Perk's home life growing up. He was bright and industrious but had very few advantages. He was frustrated. He didn't have a vision of improving his life chances at age 19. He decided to quit college and join the Army.

"In my judgment, he has the potential to become an outstanding student," I said. "His goal is to earn a degree in business. I propose he be admitted on probation to demonstrate his ability to succeed academically."

Dean Kelso disagreed.

"It will be impossible for him to make up the automatic failing grades from his past record and still make reasonable progress toward a degree," he countered. "Given his background and experience, if he can demonstrate strong academic potential, we could disallow acceptance of his record from Illinois which means he could start from scratch to meet the criteria for acceptance into the College of Business."

Dean Stuit interjected: "Given his age and background, there may be good reasons to make an exception in his case, but I would like the dean of the College of Business to agree if we're going to do this," he said.

Dean Rhodes asked me to get in touch with College of Business Dean B.L. "Bill" Barnes to explain Perk's situation.

I then met with Dean Barnes, a plain-talking Texan, with a calculator-like mind, and told Perk's story again, lobbying the dean to consider Perk if he showed success in pre-business courses in the College of Liberal Arts.

Dean Barnes was impressed by Perk's background and the way he was going about trying to achieve a degree in business. "He's just the kind of person we want to admit for increasing the numbers of minorities in business fields," Dean Barnes said. He became a major advocate for Perk as he went through the College of Business.

It was the first admissions decision I got based on criteria beyond standard grades, class rank, and undergraduate college test scores. I was confident Perk's human qualities were exceptional and he would succeed despite his record. He became my test case to demonstrate that academic potential can and does exist in students who lack the academic record for standard admissions considerations.

That was a victory, but I made it clear to Perk the work was only beginning.

"This is a tough proposal," I told him. "If you make it, you're in. If you don't, you're out after one semester or two. I made this proposal because I know you can do it. And nothing beats a failure but a try."

Perk didn't mind.

"All I want is a chance," he said. "I'm ready to get my act together – like you did."

I knew my proposal wouldn't be a problem for Perk, but I wanted to establish credibility for acceptance of my judgment – even when the obvious facts in a case defied the practices of the bureaucracy.

Perk had an outstanding undergraduate career. In three-and-a half years, he was scheduled to graduate with a degree in business administration. Because of his age – Perk was thirty-two – and the law of diminishing returns, I advised Perk to go to graduate school.

I never thought about that," he said. "I just thought I'd go get a job and start to make some money."

With encouragement from Dean Barnes, Perk applied to several top-tier MBA programs and to his surprise gained admission to the University of Chicago Booth School of Business. His confidence soared, and he accepted the offer.

Perk returned to Chicago and earned his MBA. After a brief stint with an insurance company in Connecticut, he began a meteoric rise on Wall Street. He was a financial analyst for the container industry first at Morgan Stanley, then at First Boston and finally at Goldman Sachs. In the '80s, Perk's peers elected him multiple times to the All-America Research Team – Institutional Investor magazine's exclusive annual ranking of the nation's best analysts. The magazine ranked him the country's number-one financial analyst in his field two years in a row.

The kid from the projects and one-time college dropout retired as an equity holder from Goldman Sachs at age sixty. Dean Gary Fethke selected Perk to deliver the commencement address at the College of Business commencement in 2003. On behalf of the Iowa Board of Regents and the University administration, I had the honor of conferring degrees at that commencement.

Recruiting Graduate and Professional Students

Graduate college admissions policies in general are based on a defined set of quantifiable criteria. Specific graduate departments and programs, on the other hand, may use subjective and usually more complex criteria for deciding candidates' academic potential for admissions. While taking the Graduate Record Exam (GRE) is generally required, the level of acceptable student performance varies by discipline and department.

Faculty members usually do graduate recruiting. As a result, they tend to answer questions about applicants' acceptable levels of performance and intellectual ability – answers that may be based on the department's aspirations for impressive national rankings. At Iowa, some departments were aggressive about seeking out high-potential candidates of color. Others were skeptical about admitting students who didn't demonstrate established academic criteria, even though the role of cultural bias in standardized tests was and is widely accepted in academia. That bias is a large reason why students of color often show more academic potential than their test scores indicate. I expanded my recruiting role to advocate for Black students that I felt could succeed in a given graduate program. I focused on these applicants' distinct human characteristics, life circumstances, intellectual potential, and work ethic to transcend the standard criteria of the admissions process.

Alvin Scaff, associate dean of the UI's Graduate College, was a soft-spoken sociologist and a great ally for the EOP during its early days. One day, he called me into his office to tell me he wanted to start a process to encourage graduate faculty to find promising students of color for their masters and doctorate degree programs.

"I'd like your input to help coordinate the efforts between the graduate college and academic departments," he told me.

The first student Dean Scaff brought to my attention was a shy Black woman from a small private southern HBCU. She had the grades for graduate college consideration, but her GRE scores were considerably lower than the highly competitive English master's program required. She had written an exceptionally convincing personal statement about her life experiences: She worked to pay for college because she received no help from her parents who had several younger children they supported with her father's low income. No one in her family had ever gone to college.

The Department of English decided to admit her on a trial basis. I called her to explain the risk involved in her decision to travel to Iowa City.

"I understand this isn't a guaranteed admission to the program, but I really want to have the opportunity to try," she told me. "I know I have to work hard to meet their standards, but I know I can do it If I have a chance. If I have some financial help, I'm willing to try because I have faith that I can accomplish my goals in graduate school."

She was right. She received some financial support through the EOP. Initially she struggled, but in time she completed the Master of Arts degree program.

Iowa's College of Education had no Black faculty and few Black students. Dean Howard Jones appointed two faculty members – Professor N. Peggy Burke in women's physical education and Paul Retish in special education to initiate EOP admissions for the college. While both professors were white, they were also vocal opponents of discrimination. Professor Burke was active in gender equity issues and demonstrated a cultural understanding of and comfort dealing with racial issues – probably due in part to her southern background. Professor Retish hailed from New York City and fought anti-Semitism and racial discrimination wherever he spotted it.

Along with Peggy and Paul, I attended an initial meeting with Dean Jones. He asked us to review potential minority applicants for consideration to the graduate program. We were to use our judgment – based on our assessment of their backgrounds in teaching or other professional work experience as well as their life experiences to make recommendations to various departments' admissions committees.

The first two candidates had earned bachelor's degrees from Iowa. The graduate college held their application files because neither reached the thresholds set by the faculty in their chosen programs in the College of Education. The first student was from Galesburg, Illinois, and had a degree in English education. He had been a scholarship athlete in basketball and baseball. After graduation, he played in the minor leagues and was selected in the Major League baseball draft, but an injury cut short his career. He decided to return to Iowa to pursue a graduate degree in education.

When we met to discuss his record, I pointed out his sound undergraduate record, which was exceptional, given that Black male college athletes at major universities rarely majored in such areas as English. Professor Burke agreed, and she was familiar with the student.

"I believe he is a person of strong character based on his interactions with male and female athletes," she said, before Professor Retish chimed in:

"I think it's important for us to recognize that as an athlete at his level, he had two full-time jobs, one as a student in a demanding academic major, and another as a varsity athlete in two highly competitive sports," he said.

The other candidate was a former Iowa football player. He was from East St. Louis, Illinois, and had a degree in physical education. He was married with two small children during his undergraduate studies. He had been out of college for two or three years by the time he applied for graduate college admission. During college, and after graduation, he had held a variety of jobs. He had played semi-pro football in Davenport, Iowa. When he applied for the master's program in rehabilitation counseling, Iowa Vocational Rehabilitation Services had appointed him to work with people who had disabilities.

This time, it was Professor Retish who knew the student.

"He is uniquely qualified for this program," Paul said. "He has life experiences from an economically disadvantaged community and has demonstrated great initiative and staying power to overcome adverse life circumstances. And most of all, his diverse experiences are needed in the state of Iowa."

Both men were admitted to their respective programs, and Willie "Fred" Mims and Orville "Speedy" Townsend became the UI College of Education's first EOP graduate students. Townsend built a successful career in Iowa City, rising to a senior supervisory position with Iowa Vocational Rehabilitation Services and serving as an adjunct professor in the UI's Rehabilitation Counseling program. Fred Mims also stayed in Iowa City, retiring in 2015 from his more than thirty-year career with the University Athletics Department. In that time, he became associate athletic director in charge of student services and compliance with NCAA regulations.

Graduate and professional colleges began to recognize and consider the personal qualities of exceptional minority candidates. There was an acceptance of my role for providing subjective assessments of outstanding minority candidates. I felt that my role was taken seriously by the dean of the college.

The actions of such national associations as the American Association of Medical Colleges (AAMC) in the wake of social change brought about by the Civil Rights Movement also motivated professional colleges. Colleges of medicine across the country initiated programs to correct the gross underrepresentation of Black and Latino individuals in the medical profession. As deans of the UI's College of Medicine, Dr. Robert Hardin and later Dr. Jack Eckstein were instrumental in establishing the EOP for graduate medical students. In the late 1960s and early 1970s, the dean of the College of Medicine created a subcommittee similar to the one I had served on for the College of Education.

The dean of the College of Medicine asked me to work with the EOP subcommittee to assist in recruiting. My role advocating for applicants was based on my ability to build alliances with graduate and medical faculty and academic administrators. I had an opportunity to earn respect and trust in my judgment and opinions to build confidence among committee members to admit African Americans.

The medical school EOP subcommittee didn't admit students directly, but rather screened applicants and studied their backgrounds for unique life experiences that indicated exceptional motivation and ability. Senior faculty from the basic sciences program and clinical studies, such as Richard "Dick" Kaplan from dermatology and Maurice Van Allen from neurology, comprised the committee. Dick stressed intellectual curiosity in broad humanistic terms, while Maurice looked for signs of sound academic achievement in relation to MCAT (Medical College Admissions Test) scores from both Black and brown students in medicine. The committee members never condescended in their appraisal of applicants, although they often looked to me for indigenous descriptions of some students' life experiences related to economically and educationally disadvantaged backgrounds. Once again, I was traveling between both sides of the veil.

There was a potential candidate in military service who exemplified the characteristics of a person with excellent potential but an insufficient academic record. His name is Donald Johnson. He was a thirteen-year serviceman in the U.S. Navy working as a research assistant at the Bethesda Naval Hospital. He was married and had a family. He graduated from Jackson State University in Jackson, Mississippi, with a degree in biology. His grades were average in college and he didn't do well on the MCAT.

He was referred to me by a family member who worked with Donald at Bethesda. Donald told me that at this point in his life he had just about given up his dream to become a physician. He said, "I joined the Navy to get an opportunity to better myself and serve my country. I got into medical research with the hope that I'd be able to advance toward my goal of going to medical school."

Donald's dream reflected the hope expressed in the Langston Hughes poem,

Hold fast to dreams for if dreams die life is a broken-wing bird that cannot fly.

Donald was eligible to be discharged from the Navy within the next year. He decided to apply for admissions consideration for the next academic year.

The committee had an extensive and thorough discussion about risks of admitting someone with unclear academic readiness for the rigors of the basic sciences curriculum in the first two years of medical school study.

"I think this fellow has an exceptional record of experience, but it wouldn't be fair to throw him into intense academic competition without consideration for how long he's been away from serious academic study," Dr. Van Allen said. "While it may be a difficult decision for him to make about being slowed down at his age, I think we should consider giving him a chance to get adjusted by allowing him two years to complete the first-year program."

Donald started medical school in 1972. He performed so well during the first summer that he confused the planners of his program. He performed at or near honors levels in the basic sciences courses and completed all of the courses, rather than half as had been planned, during the first and second years. He graduated in four years and went on to specialize in gastroenterology. In 2008, he returned to campus to celebrate his 30th class reunion, and to express his appreciation for the opportunity provided him to fulfill his dream. Donald has established a foundation to help disadvantaged young people.

I had a great sense of personal fulfillment to see students like Donald have an opportunity to fulfill their dreams. They didn't need a handout only a hand to get started to beat the odds of disadvantages.

70

Chapter Five:

"I'll be Colored Every Day"

One Tuesday morning in mid-September during my first semester on campus, I received a phone call from Darrell Wyrick, president of the University of Iowa Foundation. I hadn't met Darrell during my scheduled visits with each dean and didn't know much about the foundation. Except for church offerings, philanthropy wasn't part of my experience.

"We have a potential major donor who would like to consider what the University is doing for minority people," Darrell said after a brief introduction. "He's going to be on campus for the home football game this weekend. Vice President (Sandy) Boyd suggested I give you a call to see if you would be available to come to the press box during halftime to meet the donor, Roy Carver."

"Yes, I'd be happy to," I replied.

"Good," Darrell said. "I'll arrange to have a pass waiting for you at the pass gate at the stadium."

While his tone was invitational and optional, I sensed this was a command performance.

I went to Iowa Stadium – since renamed after famed Hawkeye Nile Kinnick – and up the tower elevator to the sixth level above the field-level seats. I had never been to a stadium press box. I expected to walk into a palatial setting – something like a movie set. The view was a picturesque panorama of green and gold tinged treetops, dotted with campus buildings behind a glass wall of hospital facilities. Below the press box window was a broad expanse of stadium seating for more than 60,000 spectators. The long rectangular room had several tiered rows of folding chairs facing the broad glass windows above the playing field with "HAWKEYES" stenciled into the sod at the field's north end zone and "IOWA" stenciled into the south end zone.

Against the back wall of the sparsely decorated space was a sumptuous buffet of hot and cold meats and condiments, salads, breads, desserts, and a variety of

71

soft drinks, surrounded by a display of black and gold paper napkins next to and surrounding an attractive floral arrangement. The smiling and laughing men and women mingling in the room were clad in black and gold. I had never been to a football half-time celebration, and I was surprised by the splendid and expansive party buffet.

I became acutely aware that I was the only Black person in the press box. I displayed a cool exterior, but my feelings were conflicted, embodying what W.E.B Du Bois defined as "double consciousness" – the concept that Black people live in two worlds, one inside a veil and another outside of it. Inside the veil reflects expressions within the Black vernacular experience. The reality of the Black experience in white society is reflected through perceptions from outside the veil of Black experience. This experience was outside the veil for me.

I'd never contemplated creating social change as part of an informal social setting outside the veil. Yet, here I was in a convivial setting of white people committed to the financial, political, and social advancement of the University. In a literal sense, the Black protest movement of the '60s was conducted inside the veil where Black folk functioned beyond the purview of white folk. The EOP movement, as an extension of the protest movement to create social change, was being developed outside the veil in concert with whites. I recognized that my role was in conjunction with the broader society outside the veil.

A smiling man wearing black horn-rimmed glasses approached me and introduced himself as Darrell Wyrick.

"Glad you could join us," he said. "I want you to meet and talk to Roy Carver from Muscatine [a city about forty miles southeast of Iowa City]. He's thinking about making a major gift to the university, and one of the areas he'd like to learn about is the MLK Scholarship Program."

I tried to form an impression of the sturdily built, more than 6-foot tall middle-aged Roy Carver with a brownish gray crew cut, wearing glasses, and an affable expression that seemed to be expecting me. I had imagined he'd be like the stern-faced men in dark suits carrying thin briefcases in the financial district I used to see when I worked at Toffenetti's Restaurant in high school. They represented what I imagined rich men looked like.

Carver didn't fit the image I had formed looking out from behind the veil into the world on the other side.

He was pleasant during our brief introduction but shifted to all business about the meeting and the impending conversation.

"I'm pleased to meet you, Mr. Carver," I said as we settled into the seats.

"Call me Roy," he politely interrupted. "Do you go by Phil?"

I nodded my head, trying to get comfortable with being on a first-name basis with the man who founded and ran the Bandag Corporation for retreading tires. His offices were housed in a plain brick one-story building in an industrial section of Muscatine.

"Tell me about your program. I'd like to know what you do and how it's working out," he inquired.

I summarized the goals of the program and outlined where I'd gone and where I intended to go to visit high schools in Iowa.

"Have you been to Muscatine?" he asked.

I mused slightly at my difficulty trying to get the attention of Muscatine's high school administrators, so I could meet with the city's large population of Mexican American students. Fort Madison, an hour south of Muscatine, was previously a switching point for the Santa Fe Railroad. For years Mexican Americans working on the railroad had settled in Muscatine, as had migrant farm workers – some of whom picked and processed tomatoes for Heinz.

Thanks to encouragement from one of his sons, Roy Carver was looking to understand the goals and functions of the University's efforts, so he could determine whether the program met his high standards of involvement and financial support.

"Since I'd like to see what you do, you could come to Muscatine and meet with the students in my office," Carver offered. "If you don't mind, I'll call the high school and invite the counselors and students. Phil, you tell me what your schedule is like, and I'll arrange a time."

I was flabbergasted! His comment deflated my image of Roy Carver as an aloof, rich white guy.

He scheduled the meeting and I drove to Muscatine on a bright autumn morning during the early fall semester. Roy Carver's office was a long, narrow room with a large rectangular conference table surrounded by a dozen chairs that gave the impression the room was even narrower.

Seated at the conference table were seven olive-complexioned young people, four females and three males, and their white school counselors. The room had a polite but uncomfortable feeling to me. The counselors had shown little interest in encouraging Mexican American students to go to the University of Iowa and had ignored my previous recruiting inquiries. Their tune changed when the overture came from a prominent local industrialist requesting essentially a command performance.

"Thank you, students and counselors too, for agreeing to allow me the opportunity to sit in on your meeting with University of Iowa Admissions Officer Phil Jones, who is helping the University of Iowa offer opportunities for you to go to college," Carver said in his plain midwestern dialect.

The students were quietly polite yet unresponsive, but most shared a glimmer in their eyes as I presented. I had the feeling they showed up because they were told to, but I think upon arrival they realized that there was a genuine opportunity to go beyond high school other than, or in addition to, going to the local community college in Muscatine.

Carver sat in a chair slightly away from the conference table. His vantage point allowed him to see the facial expressions of the students as well as mine. His engagement in the conversation was clear despite his silence. I detected approval from his body language. After I handed out the recruiting literature and began to engage the students in conversation – though they were mostly silent – he questioned them individually about how they liked school and if they thought it was a good idea for the University to offer scholarships to students like them. As several students warmed to his overtures, their facial expressions and body postures relaxed.

"I think this is something worthwhile," Carver said to me once the students and counselors left. "I'm glad you gave me a chance to learn about what you're doing to create this program. I appreciate you taking the time to come down today to help me understand the picture."

That was the last thing he said to me for more than two years. In that time, as I learned to navigate the University's landscape, I spoke to Darrell Wyrick frequently – though never about the Carver meeting.

In November 1971 about thirty-six months after my visit to Carver's office, I was listening to the University of Iowa's radio station, WSUI. I heard the announcer read news of a University of Iowa Foundation press conference scheduled for that morning in the Senate Chamber of Old Capitol to unveil a major gift to the University from none other than Roy J. Carver.

It was about nine o'clock in the morning. My pulse quickened. My thoughts rushed back to Darrell Wyrick's initial comments about Carver's interest in the MLK Scholarship Program. In the three years since then, I'd become director of the Department of Special Support Services. My instinctive response was to go immediately to Old Capitol.

It was a gray, chilly morning as I walked from my Gilmore Hall office across the Pentacrest toward Old Capitol. I had no tangible basis for this impulse, yet I felt like a child on Christmas about to open a surprise present. I continued to do as my mother always told me: "Follow your mind."

My sense of excitement was reminiscent of the feelings I experienced three years earlier. As I opened the heavy ornate doors to the Old Capitol, I remembered my first time entering the building when I came to campus in May 1968 to interview for my recruiting position. I met with President Bowen in what was originally the office of Iowa's first governor. It later housed Vice President for Academic Affairs Willard "Sandy" Boyd and Dean of Academic Affairs Philip G. Hubbard.

I climbed the circular stairs to the second floor and turned toward the open door leading into the room. Chandeliers above the Senate Chamber illuminated the room; it was sparsely filled with members of the media setting up TV cameras behind three rows of five chairs each. Several people, probably foundation staff, mingled near a podium at the front of the room next to three chairs – presumably for Roy Carver and the presidents of the university and the foundation.

I spotted Roy Carver among those mingling, and when he looked up and saw me surveying the room from the open doorway, he smiled broadly and raised an arm calmly but deliberately beckoning me.

"Wow – he recognized me," I thought. "My instincts may be right."

In my gray Navy pea-coat, covering my gray wool turtleneck sweater and a pair of dark slacks, I had the sensation I wasn't dressed appropriately for the occasion. Undeterred, I went over to join Roy Carver and the others standing alongside the podium.

As I approached him, Roy Carver smiled broadly and extended his hand to shake mine. His hand was broadly muscular and shaking it felt like having my hand wrapped in a pound of spare ribs.

"Hello, Phil, glad to see you," he said as he looked in the direction of a reporter with a camera and a notebook.

Carver called to the reporter from the Omaha Herald, "Could you come over here for a moment to take a picture of us, please?"

As the reporter got ready, Carver positioned himself between Darrell Wyrick and me and leaned over to speak softly in my ear. He said, with pride in his voice, "I told you I was going to do something for the colored boys."

Then as now, the term "colored boys" was not in vogue. Despite the militancy of the Black Consciousness Movement in the '60s that railed against use of the terms "Negro" and "colored," I didn't feel offended by Roy Carver's words. Unlike the contempt I felt when the restaurant owner in Champaign told me he didn't want colored people in his place, I sensed genuine warmth in Carver's comment and the embrace of his hand on my shoulder felt like a true transfer of positive emotion.

His initial gift to the University of Iowa in 1971 provided an endowment initially valued at two hundred fifty thousand dollars to support equal opportunity programs. Over the years I've described my feelings as, "For that kind of money I'll be 'colored' every day."

During intervening years, we used the Carver funds to support the disadvantaged in various ways – ranging from scholarships to establishing a summer program for EOP medical students, to reinforce a summer experience for gifted high school students of color, to participate in the Belin-Blank Center for the Gifted and Talented at the University of Iowa, and other causes consistent with Carver's initial wishes. He did more than just something for the "colored boys" and girls.

Left, Phillip Jones; Center, donor, Roy J. Carver; Right, UI Foundation President, Darrell D. Wyrick

Chapter Six:

Epiphany

EOP directors often had ideological struggles without power, insight, or resources to resolve system issues. We knew well the traumas of racial discrimination – overt and subtle – that Blacks historically experienced on predominantly white campuses because most of us lived through them as students. We had a passion to solve student problems case by case. I learned, however, that passion isn't enough to change a system.

Because my position was unstructured, I frequently improvised to get things done properly. I discovered the Sisyphean tasks of confronting a complex institution without a competent understanding of financial management, business procedures, or academic and administrative regulations.

My thoughts were frequently confused, and my mind was in constant turmoil about what I perceived as individual resistance from other administrators and faculty to the EOP and me personally. With little success, I reviewed student development journals and books. I went to several conferences where I learned about similar constraints, which wasn't surprising since most of us had similar backgrounds and other institutions had the same problems.

I learned about a grant program for a training institute for creating social change in higher education sponsored by the Wright Institute in Berkeley, California. I was intrigued by the thought of a five-week program to study institutional change initiatives in colleges and universities. I applied and gained acceptance in January 1969

Nevitt Sanford, a professor of psychology at Stanford University, headed the Wright Institute. I learned about his 1968 book, Where Colleges Fail, which emphasizes that colleges tend to falter when they treat students as commodities rather than people.

The two militant program directors espoused an anti-establishment political agenda. Their philosophy was based on the premise that the establishment only yields to external social pressures. They believed student protests were the vehicle for creating social change to gain equality of opportunity for disadvantaged student access and financial support.

While I understood their position, I knew there was more to creating substantive change than simply having a demonstration every time there needed to be a policy change for EOP. They tended to emphasize the radical elements of the California programs we studied. We learned a lot about what was wrong with the administrators or power brokers who resisted change, but we didn't hear from established administrators who held the power in the institutions. My experience at the institute helped me lay the foundation to visualize and articulate the basis for developing a proposal to create a university support service department to administer EOP.

When I started at Iowa, Don Rhodes told me, "Every campus is different, and what applies in one environment may not translate the same way in another campus culture. You have to interpret things to fit your situation."

I called Don at the University of Oregon – where he went from Iowa – to ask if he would let me come to Eugene for a day to spend time talking to him about my ideas. "I'll be glad to look at your ideas again. I'm glad you're thinking about how to integrate what you've been doing since I asked you to develop a job description last year to start the EOP at Iowa."

After considerable conversation, he summarized his thoughts by saying, "I think your thinking has merit, but you need to gain more insight into the administrative and academic structures of the university in general and Iowa in particular, in order to create a comprehensive university service program."

I took his advice when I went back to Iowa and began my quest to gain more insight. First, I had a conversation with a faculty member named James "Jim" Dickenson, who worked part-time in the Office of Academic Affairs. Jim suggested I take a course he taught in the student development program to form a foundation for understanding the basis for student services administration. I took the course in 1970. I wrote a position paper to create a department of supportive services in the division of student services. Subsequently, I enrolled in the student development doctoral program.

When I presented my proposal to President Boyd and Vice President Hubbard in 1970, they agreed to establish a student support services department in the division of student services.

President Boyd directed: "Students should be treated like all other students, but the services should be special. Students should not be required to use the services, but support should be available for every student to the extent of their individual needs. These are special support services."

So, we named the department Special Support Services (SSS) which evolved into the Center for Diversity and Excellence. Programs in the department were designed to be distinctive and personal, to provide financial and cultural support based on individual need with the goal for students to function independently by the end of their second year.

"Students should be proud to participate in special support services to work to achieve excellence, and that should be our attitude toward each of them," Vice President Hubbard said.

Today, support services are considered appropriate for all students to achieve student success. I worry whether disadvantaged students' unique needs will receive adequate funding and cultural understanding for them to be as successful as their peers who don't face similar obstacles to increase their life chances.

My approach to establishing support services for disadvantaged minorities entering universities was shared a great deal among retention programs for at-risk students. Other EOP directors shared those tactics, and we faced resistance from critics who considered support services a crutch for unqualified students.

In 1972 I learned about another program through the U.S. Office of Education. I received a copy of the application for the 1973-74 fellowship for a short-term training program. It presented an excellent opportunity to create something I had mused about during my experiences at various national and regional gatherings of EOP directors and after attending the Wright Institute in California.

Drawing on my observations of various campuses during my stay at the Wright Institute, I wanted to structure a seminar experience coupled with a practicum that required several months on the home campuses of the participants.

The grant allowed for a four-week program. I designed a plan for a one-week residential training program at the beginning of the fiscal year in July 1973, with a fall practicum period followed by a one or two-day mid-year meeting at the College Board office in Evanston, Illinois, or the American College Testing office in Iowa City. The practicum would resume during the spring term. The program would include site visits by the program staff during the fall and spring practicums. My program would conclude with a weeklong campus in-residence training session in Iowa City at the end of the fiscal year in June 1974.

I recruited a staff of African American support services directors and educational professionals to conduct the program with me. The staff consisted of James "Jim" Baugh, EOP director at University of Wisconsin in Madison; Clara Fitzpatrick from the College Board in Evanston, Illinois; Manuel "Manny" Pierson, Dean of

Students at Oakland University in Rochester, Michigan; and Clarence Shelley, EOP director at the University of Illinois, Urbana-Champaign.

We called the program "The Iowa EOP Institute." Invitations for participation were open to EOP administrators in the Midwest who were responsible for developing comprehensive support services programs. We considered requests from outside the region to reach the fifteen to twenty-five total participants the grant allowed.

The institute's immediate objective was to increase enrollment and to foster academic success of students of color and low-income students at participating institutions through a general strengthening of EOP administrators' capabilities. My long-range objective was to develop a core of EOP professionals who were committed to initiating subsequent regional training institutes for other EOP staff members and directors.

In July 1972 I submitted the proposal for thirty thousand dollars to fund the institute. I became anxious about whether the office would accept the proposal. Clark Chipman, a program director in the Region V Office of Education in Chicago, asked me several times if I had heard anything.

"Jones, you need to go to Washington to talk up your ideas to get your proposal funded," he said. "EOP directors need to establish a presence in Washington, or you're always going to be left out of the politics and funding priorities for the disadvantaged in federal programs."

At first, I was overwhelmed by the challenge, but I felt he was right. Clark, a white, politically astute, culturally sensitive, social change advocate, constantly advised Black administrators – among others – how to negotiate the maze of regulations and political influence exerted by congressional representatives.

"It's your responsibility to sensitize the federal bureaucracy to expanding educational opportunities for Blacks in predominantly white, as well as in historically Black, colleges and universities," he told me.

In January 1973 I went to the Office of Education in Washington, D.C., to lobby for my proposal. I had some help getting started. Clark mentioned me to Dr. Leonard H. O. Spearman, Sr., director of the Division of Student Assistance, and he agreed to meet me.

Len, as I came to call him, was an outstanding educator, career bureaucrat, and Black Republican who had a lot of influence in government, which he used astutely among political appointees in the Nixon administration. A graduate of Florida A&M University, a well-known historically Black school, Len was committed to increasing funding for student assistance in developing institutions including HBCUs. Although it was not in his division, Leonard agreed to listen to my proposal because it might help raise the level of the TRIO future funding that he administered.

Like my trip to the West Coast, I felt that my journey to Washington would be equally trans-formative. On my flight, I wondered about the institute's possible impact on higher education. As the plane descended across Chesapeake Bay toward the D.C. runway, my thoughts turned to the majesty of the Washington Monument, west end of the National Mall, and the U.S. Capitol at the east end.

It was sobering to see these landmarks now as I was thinking about my desire to create social change through organizational development. My eyes were upon the site where Dr. King led hundreds of thousands in a march to transform the nation in 1963, the genesis of strides toward equity in many areas – including higher education. The fact that I, a kid from the projects on the south side of Chicago, was in Washington, D.C., to propose a program to create social change produced in me a sense of awe and anxiety.

The Office of Education's building is on the northwest corner of D at Seventh Street Southwest. The entrance to the General Services Administration building is plain and unadorned. The elevator and hallways had an industrial quality, completely unlike what I had imagined, but with an atmosphere ripped from the stereotypes of faceless bureaucracy: long, institutionally green walls, and a phalanx of doors with frosted glass windows, that reminded me of the old IBM computer punch card.

I came to a corner office door marked, "Division of Student Assistance, Dr. Leonard Spearman, Deputy Assistant Commissioner of Education." In a bright reception office, I was greeted by a friendly cocoa-colored woman who greeted me as if we'd already met. She escorted me past several windowless offices equipped with comfortable looking older furniture to a large corner office filled with sunlight reflecting off an impressive collection of plaques, commendations, and framed photographs.

Entering the office, I was met by the assistant commissioner – a stylishly dressed, tall, muscular, sepia colored man wearing a modest salt-and-pepper Afro. His warm greeting, radiant smile, firm handshake, and air of confidence along with the receptionist's familiar smile made me feel at ease.

"Thank you, Dr. Spearman, for taking time to see me," I said.

"Glad to do it. Please call me Len," he replied. In a familiar vernacular he said, "Clark has told me some good things about what you all are trying to accomplish out there in the Midwest."

"Thank you," I said. "I'd like to get your advice and possibly your assistance, for a project I've proposed for a training institute for special program administrators."

We sat at his conference table as I outlined my proposal for funding the EOP Institute. Len listened attentively, his eyes revealing his positive reception to the concept.

"I think this is just the kind of thinking we need to advance initiatives around the country to increase disadvantaged student enrollments and graduation rates," he said.

Reflexively, his tone shifted from vernacular to didactic, bringing to my mind Ralph Ellison's groundbreaking novel Invisible Man. I imagined Ellison's description of President Bledsoe's tones when he was instructing the Black male college student about how to conduct himself in interacting with influential white people. I sensed a cultural message to conduct myself with professional poise, confidence, and eloquence much as I had been taught growing up about how to comport myself with white people.

Len instructed me that the Title 5E programs, which the EOP Institute would be part of, weren't in his division. He summoned his office assistant and asked her to find out who managed the Title 5E programs.

She left and returned shortly to notify us that Dr. John Peo was the person we were looking for. His office was on the same floor in a different wing of the building.

"We'll call ahead to set up an appointment while you walk around there – and when you finish, come back here to let me know what you find out," Len said.

Excited and exhilarated, I hurried through the labyrinth of corridors. Dr. Peo's office was a broad windowless room drenched in florescent lighting. John, as he asked for me to call him, was a middle-aged, brown-haired man who looked like he spent most of his time indoors. He expected me, and he had a manila folder with Iowa written on a sticker on his desk. After we introduced ourselves, he got right down to business.

"We've received your proposal, and we can discuss any questions you've got," he said.

"Since it's been quite a while since I submitted it, and I still hadn't heard anything, I thought I'd come in to learn if the application was incomplete or if a decision had been made about it," I said. Like Len, John listened attentively. Unfortunately,

John had much more of a poker face. I responded by beginning to pitch him my proposal.

He listened patiently as I emoted and gesticulated dramatically to display my passion for my ideas. His body language and facial expression indicated interest. With practiced style, he moved his hands toward the folder. I soon learned it held my proposal.

"Your proposal has been reviewed and didn't get a favorable rating from a panel of educators, many of whom were from historically Black colleges," he said, each word stinging more than the last. "They thought it might be from predominantly white faculty to train minority administrators at their institutions."

My heart began to pound. His statements were like blows to my sternum. My mouth tasted dry as I tried to regain my composure – relying on a lifetime's worth of lessons about displaying poise and being articulate – especially in dealing with influential white folks.

I knew exactly what was on the reviewers' minds. It was not uncommon for white folks to coopt Black folks' ideas to benefit themselves. I think the Black reviewers saw the funding as an attempted rip-off of Black folks' initiatives.

The cogency of my proposal raised the specter of the precept of white superiority and Black inferiority. Black reviewers probably presumed the comprehensive nature of the proposal was beyond the scope of Black administrators new to predominantly white universities. Therefore, Black reviewers probably presumed that whites must have written it.

I looked directly at Dr. Peo with a confident smile.

"From what I've told you, I think you can see that these proposals are my ideas," I said, remembering to show deference. "I conceived them. I developed them. I wrote them."

Dr. Peo's face softened, revealing sympathy. My proposal's humanity seemed to resonate with him, though his tone and disposition conveyed that he could not contradict the Black administrators who negatively reviewed my proposal.

He offered a solution:

"Since your proposal may not have been entirely clear to the review panel, you should submit an addendum to clarify the question about cooperative sponsorships. Your original description may have left the impression that the institute was being conducted by someone other than you and your EOP colleagues."

I realized how tense I'd been as my fingers loosened their grip on the arms of my chair. I thanked him and shook his hand firmly as I left his office to return to Len.

Len was pleased by Dr. Peo's suggestion and reached for his phone. After momentary small talk, he said, "Willa, I've got a young man in my office who has submitted a proposal for Part E grant funding from your division. I think he has some innovative ideas that might interest you. If you've got a few minutes, I'd like to ask if you can spend a few minutes with him to share his thoughts with you."

"Good," he said, nodding affirmatively. "I'll send him down right away. I appreciate it."

Dr. Willa Player was Len's peer and a relatively new Republican presidential appointee. Previously, she had been president of the small, historically Black Bennett College in Greensboro, North Carolina.

Dr. Player was a stately looking, middle-aged woman with a mahogany complexion and an elegant coiffured hairstyle. She invited me into her office, and I gave her a brief overview of my proposal.

"Your ideas seem to offer some interesting and innovative approaches," she said. "I encourage you to send the addendum to Dr. Peo as soon as possible, as he requested." She appeared to carefully avoid making any judgments or to imply acceptance or rejection of my ideas.

I reported back to Len's office. After a few minutes of quiet contemplation, he said: "You go home and take care of the proposal, and I'll take care of the politics."

On January 15, 1973, I submitted my addendum to Dr. John Peo. Three weeks later, I received approval of the application to fund the University of Iowa Training Institute for the development of EOP administrators. I breathed a huge sigh of relief.

I learned firsthand the significance of relationships building to create social change. The old boys' network is often correctly perceived to perpetuate white-male dominance thus excluding minorities and women from professional advancement. I may have been naïve, but it seemed counterintuitive to expect that expanding opportunities for people of color would rely upon the same process.

I learned that building personal and professional relationships isn't inherently racially biased though individuals in institutions often expect it to be such. Knowing the right people is an important way to develop alliances and create support. Many decisions, not just in education, are made by committees. Building coalitions serves players well. My trip to Washington was an introduction to forming alliances to create social change.

Being ingratiated felt good. It was encouraging and instructive to me that we, as Black people, could have more confidence that we could be treated more fairly in the nationwide network of referrals and endorsements.

I am proud of what was accomplished by the fifteen participants in the institute. They represented a diverse group of colleges and universities. To preserve the record, my former colleague, Vice President for Publications at the American College Testing Program (ACT) Ted Molen, published a monograph of the institute's six seminar speaker presentations which centered on the historical development, contemporary, continuing, and future issues related to increasing educational opportunities for all Americans in postsecondary education. In an era of instant history, the monograph was meant to place the development of EOP in a historical context.

Hugh Lane, president of the National Scholarship Service and Fund for Negro Students (NSSFNS), closed the seminar presentations with a challenging admonition:

"The director of EOP is a crucial part of the educational process. Some tension is implicit in that assumption. The extent to which the interaction can be carried out from the position of EOP director is also a measure of the extent to which the EOP functions as an integral part of the educational process."

I invited Leonard Spearman to the second summer session on the University of Iowa campus. He spent two days interacting with the institute's staff. His behavior reminded me of some professor quizzing graduate students during thesis defenses. Len was exacting in his analysis and demonstrated both agreement and disagreement with various points. After the presentations, the staff took Len to dinner.

He smiled broadly as he greeted each of the five of us with a hardy handshake and bear hug. With vernacular rhythm displaying shades of his background as a saxophonist in the Florida A&M Jazz Band – he tapped the table with his right index finger, while holding a highball glass of scotch and water in the other hand, he said:

"You all have created exactly the kind of training we need across this country to develop more support to increase federal funding for programs for the disadvantaged."

His eyes brightened, and he spread his arms majestically:

"I've got a great idea about how to start the process," he continued emphatically.

After the conclusion of the institute in the fall of 1974, Len announced the formation of the National Task Force on the Disadvantaged and Postsecondary Education. The commission was composed of thirty-three people from around the country including me from inside and outside the federal government.

The following January, Len presented recommendations to U.S. Commissioner of Education Terrell H. Bell. Included among the fifteen recommendations was that "The federal government should sponsor activities designed to increase the effectiveness of programs through the development and training of staff... to develop competencies and knowledge related specifically to the needs of disadvantaged clientele."

The recommendations were adopted and funded as the training authority for TRIO staff development nationwide. The Iowa EOP institute served as the prototype for what became the national training program for TRIO administrators.

Chapter Seven:

Transition

The conclusion of the institute marked the end of an important phase in my career. In 1974 I completed my doctorate. Using data from the institute, I developed a descriptive analysis of the administrative structures of EOPs for my dissertation. It also included an analysis of principles in a broader context emphasizing human rights, freedom of expression, and student rights and responsibilities. A wise comment from Sandy Boyd at the final session of the institute served as my thesis:

"In my interpretation of everything that is happening, and has happened in this country in recent years, and indeed throughout the world, the driving force in the world today is obviously equality of opportunity. Those who have not had opportunity to participate in the past are going to participate now and in the future. One of those opportunities for participation is in education."

I pondered what I would do in my future. I tend to approach personal problems academically, that is, by finding as much information I can and then synthesizing all possibilities. Regardless of how many options you have, you can only walk in one direction at a time. I believe in being as consistent as the information I have. I don't have a problem changing my mind when I get new insights.

My dilemma was whether I should stay in Iowa or look for another position at an institution with more Black people. We had been in Iowa more than the five years I originally thought we'd stay, but its lack of diversity left much to be desired. I struggled with whether we should raise our children in a primarily white community. In both Chicago and Flint, I became frustrated and depressed by my inability to impact changes to improve the life chances of people in the Black communities.

I wanted to have a greater impact than on a case by case basis. I thought there are no perfect situations, so I decided to follow the adage to grow where you're planted. I felt I was in a better position to affect social change and to affect the life chances of Black students in the University than I might have somewhere else.

I also was faced with the lack of professional respect for those of us working in EOP, as well as the general low status other administrators at major universities conferred upon us student affairs professionals. I juxtaposed my opposing views about facing my future in higher education. I framed the decision as one of choosing the best opportunity for developing EOP components – both at the institution I worked in as well as in the wider context of higher education and society.

I felt anxious and unsure of myself. I questioned assumptions I had made about my role in furthering opportunities for Black students.

With more knowledge and insight about the culture and administrative functions of major universities, I began to question, how to expand the concept of disadvantaged student programs to include equitable support for all students.

I had a feeling of frustration whenever I considered my ideal in the context of my everyday reality: Without enough financial and human resources, compounded by the fact that economically poor and educationally disadvantaged students constituted less than three percent of the University of Iowa's total student population, we could never achieve true equity or anything close to it.

Over time, I observed that Iowa didn't function like the vertical organizational charts that typically depict university administrations. Academic departments don't operate entirely, as history would suggest, like a community of scholars. There's quite a bit of individual entrepreneurial competition among faculty in search of funding opportunities for their own research. Furthermore, there's an administrative overlay that controls space, equipment, facilities, services and financial resources.

President Boyd often said, "People, not structures, make great institutions." The university was a maze of complex coalitions with interrelated competing interests. Expertise was widely diffused. Different people had modicums of power in varying areas of administrative control.

Rather than a vertical structure, where power and decision-making are vested in a single administrator in a leading managerial position, I found that I had to talk to and work with a variety of people to get a situation resolved for a student.

Achieving educational outcomes at Iowa tends to be characterized by two-way horizontal organizational communication rather than one-way vertical reporting typically associated with bureaucracies. It takes an alliance among individuals with modicums of power to effect organizational change in a university – Iowa included.

In developing the proposal to create the Department of Special Support Services during my first two years, I accepted the challenge of building alliances to increase financial and programmatic support for creating social change through organizational development. I was aware that I, and practically all other EOP directors, were part of non-academic student personnel services and student development that was in a state of flux and not necessarily highly regarded or even understood by members of our changing profession or the faculty.

The responsibilities for student affairs and services in the 1960s had risen to the vice-presidential level in many major universities. Student affairs professionals were frequently characterized as people-oriented, not generally aggressive or assertive and uncomfortable in administrative roles – behaviors that are not necessarily rewarded in the administrative arena where ability to take initiative to work with peers often determines success.

In response to Black students' social activism, the role of an EOP director evolved, and necessitated confidence and assertiveness to create social change. That behavior was in direct contrast to the overall characterization of student development administrators. But to achieve social progress, EOP directors could not be passive. The lack of connection was further magnified by the fact that the American College Personnel Association and the National Association of Student Personnel Administrators, two key national student affairs organizations, were not on the forefront advocating equality of educational opportunity for Black students in the 1960s and early 1970s.

Student services administrative structures became more complex after Dixon v. Alabama State Board of Education, a federal court decision that recognized college students' right to due process in disciplinary matters. The case dealt with five Black students who participated in a civil rights demonstration and the rise of similar campus protest movements — led by students of various backgrounds for many causes – created functional ambiguity for student affairs/services personnel. The creation of disadvantaged student programs on white campuses further clouded the role.

With the combination of new experiences and insights gained from the institute and earning my doctorate degree I developed new outlooks on the university's organizational complexity as a social institution and the multi-dimensional aspects of student development. From my new perspective, I decided student services administrators have a role in initiating, interpreting, and improvising ways to provide educational experiences.

In working through my dilemma, I concluded that creating equality of educational opportunity organizationally requires more than increasing the number of Black students on campus; it requires full participation in the life of the university.

While I was satisfied that I had answered some of my questions, I still hadn't come to terms with whether to continue what I had done before finishing my degree. I felt like I was being drawn back to the Black community, yet I had developed an appreciation for the University of Iowa and the people of Iowa City.

I questioned myself about which way to go. William "Bill" Shanhouse, Iowa's vice president for administrative services, called me to outline a proposal he planned to offer the University administration. The Division of Administrative Services consisted of physical plant operations, University business office, data processing, human resources, space allocation, and the business operations of the Iowa Memorial Union (IMU) and University Housing and Dining. Through Bill's initiatives, the University created transportation and academic and personal support services for students with disabilities. And Bill was asking me to be a division vice president.

I was stunned. I had never dreamed of being a vice president. I had only pictured myself working in some type of EOP position. Because of a limited self-perception, I lacked the ability to dream big. I knew how to take initiative and stick out tough times until I achieved my goal, but I needed to expand my horizons. In that moment, I realized I had been casting my net in shallow water. I had to learn to feel as confident in my aspirations as I felt passionate about achieving equality of opportunity.

As time went by, I thought more and more about moving into an unfamiliar situation. Administrative Services was a relatively new vice-presidential area. Sandy Boyd had created the division in the early 1970s. I wasn't sure how I would fit in, and I wasn't sure I would want to stop reporting to Dean Philip Hubbard. I didn't want to be the token Black person in administrative services. After considerable thought, I decided to decline Bill's offer.

Bill wasn't deterred. He talked to President Boyd and Dean Hubbard about how he could make the position attractive to me. He asked me to meet with him again. Based on my experience working with students in EOP, my degree in student development, and my demonstrated management ability in creating and running the Special Support Services department, Bill outlined a plan to have me be a member of his staff and to report jointly to him and Dean Hubbard. I accepted the position.

In early 1975 I began my career in central administration at the University of Iowa as assistant vice president for administrative services with what I called an "improvisational portfolio."

Consequently, I did not find it unusual that my new role included input in affirmative action along with housing administration, dining services, residence hall programs, and the IMU – which included a hotel, bookstore, and retail food services. I also had an informal role providing input to the campus committee formed to respond to campus emergencies and disruptions – called the Administrative Liaison Group (ALG), chaired by Duane "Sprie" Spriestersbach, the vice president for research and dean of the graduate college.

When a reporter asked if I thought these responsibilities were given to me as a token Black appointment, I replied, "I don't know if it's tokenism. As the first Black non-faculty vice presidential appointment, I will do what I should do to achieve excellence in everything I do. Regardless of why I was appointed, if I don't produce, I know they won't let me keep the position just because I'm Black."

During my first few months in the position, President Boyd called me to come to his Monday morning cabinet meeting – a weekly gathering of the president and his vice presidents. This wasn't a new thing for me. President Boyd would periodically have me come to docket meetings to give EOP status reports. That Monday, I walked into the conference room in the president's office in Room 101 Jessup Hall to see Provost May Broadbeck, Sprie Spriestersbach, Dean Hubbard and Bill Shanhouse mid-conversation.

President Boyd looked up, paused, and said, "Come to the table Phil and have a seat."

The conference table was oval shaped with five high-back swivel chairs on either side. The arrangement spanned the length and width of the room, from the door to the windows on the other end of the room. The group was spread out around the table, with President Boyd sitting at the end of the table under the windows. He motioned for me to take the chair at the opposite end nearest the door. Without saying a word, all eyes turned in my direction with a collective quizzical gaze fixed on me.

"Phil, Cece is going to be leaving the University in June," President Boyd said, referring to Dr. Cecelia Foxley, director of affirmative action. "My colleagues and I think you should assume the responsibilities as director of affirmative action. We believe you've had a good feel for this area and would be right for the job."

Another pause, still with all eyes in my direction. "What do you think?" Sandy asked after what felt like too long.

My only thought was, "Is this another EOP situation?"

"I think this would be a good fit for you in your present position, so we could add director of affirmative action to your title as assistant vice president," Bill Shanhouse said. "It simply describes what you are already assisting with in administrative services across the University."

I saw the position as a broader tapestry to use functional coordination to create social change.

Chapter Eight:

Affirmative Fairness

I became more involved in the University's broader interpersonal complexities once I was appointed director of affirmative action. I recognized I needed to lead by earning others' trust. I came to realize that the University of Iowa is small for a large institution and large for a small institution. Interpersonal relationships matter in getting things done. To make progress in such a democratic and entrepreneurial environment, one must have a high tolerance for ambiguity. It's like a jazz composition. There's a basic structure and melody, but room for improvisation.

I was going through this metamorphosis – trying to learn how to function with a wider perspective – when I was offered an opportunity that expanded my perception of social justice. A former EOP student named Jerry Drew, who graduated from the Iowa College of Law, was working for Sister Cities International to recruit American minorities for a study tour of West Germany.

As a gift to the United States in recognition of the American bicentennial in 1976, The Institute Fur Auslandsbeziehungen hosted the study tour on behalf of the West German Government. The purpose of the study tour was for U.S. minorities to observe West German society in various cities and universities and share perspectives on racial integration in America as compared to that in West Germany.

I didn't quite know what to expect. I thought Germany was a white society. I knew Black guys who served in Germany in the military, but I didn't have a view of Germany having its own non-white residents. While jogging on my first day in Stuttgart, I encountered a dark-skinned group of men working on a street project supervised by a white man. I asked the institute director who were the dark-skinned workers and if they were discriminated against in employment.

"There's no discrimination against Black people here," I was told.

"Who are the dark-skinned people I saw working on a street crew with white supervisors?" I asked, skeptically.

"Oh, you mean the Gastarbeiter – or guest workers," the director said. A less charitable descriptor was "schwartzer," meaning "Black workers."

94

West Germany faced a labor shortage in the 1960s. Turkish laborers – like migrant workers in America – came to West Germany to fill low skill jobs. Like migrant farmworkers in America, economics forced many Turkish immigrants to live in poor quality, low income housing with inadequate education for their children.

The director explained, "There are some difficulties with the Turks. They don't speak German and are not well educated, but they are not discriminated against like what you are talking about in your country. There's a friendly atmosphere toward Black people in Germany. We don't have a critical mass of Black people from America or other parts of the world in Germany."

"You may not realize it, but you may be creating the same economic injustice and racial prejudice for the immigrants from Turkey that many low-skilled, undereducated Black and Hispanic people experience in the United States," I said, describing cultural parallels I was rapidly drawing in my head.

"Our situations are much different. The Turks came to Germany voluntarily. They may leave at any time," another member of the host group interjected defensively.

No, the guest workers weren't slaves, but their economic conditions mirrored those of Latino migrant workers in the U.S. I saw then that racial prejudice and economic deprivation go together in society, no matter the country nor continent.

I brought that lesson back to Iowa City. I tried harder, armed with more experience, to think creatively about how to merge what I learned in recruiting EOP students with creating ways to engineer economic mobility for people of color and other disadvantaged groups. I saw the Turkish guest workers as clear examples of what happens to disadvantaged people everywhere. Fundamentally, affirmative action is about fairness.

Like many in my community, growing up I had a strong sense of unfairness in society without being able to articulate it or its cause. When I was in third grade, seated two to a desk in a building so overcrowded that we went to school for half days, I heard adults complain about our conditions, but I didn't know any better or different. In 1945, when I was five years old on a train trip to Birmingham, Alabama, with my mother and sister, I remember the train stopping for a long delay. The train car began to move backward and then stopped with a jolt.

A group of Black soldiers and sailors carrying large, long, green bags slung over their shoulders came into the railroad coach laughing and talking loudly about having their own coach on the train. People already on the train joined in the jocular conversation. They offered to share with the soldiers and sailors part of the traditional traveling shoebox lunches of cold fried chicken and sliced pound cake.

I didn't know it at the time, but later in life I learned to recognize the painful twinge of irony I sensed. You learn to laugh to keep from crying. When we boarded the overnight train at Illinois Central Station on Roosevelt Road in downtown Chicago, the coach was desegregated. By the time we got to Cairo, Illinois, the southernmost point in Illinois, all the white people had left the coach. The Black people were joking about Jim Crow. I didn't know the meaning of the term, but in the tone of their voices I sensed the fundamental unfairness they must have felt. Cairo was where the train crossed from Illinois into Kentucky – the point of legal racial segregation in the South.

In 1960 when I was a twenty-year-old college student, I revisited the experience of the train trip to Birmingham. As we had done when I was a child, I took a train from the Illinois Central Station. The train was less glamorous than I remembered. It didn't have the same mystique. I remembered the ceremonial process of ticket taking from the past when the white conductor and Black porter came through the railroad car. The conductor punched tickets and announced destinations. He handed the punched ticket to the porter who clipped it above each seat. Under Jim Crow, porters took directions from conductors.

They wore identical uniforms, except for gold buttons on conductor uniforms and silver buttons for porters who were responsible for putting up and taking down luggage from overhead racks. They brought pillows through the train cars at night for passengers to rent, and they were attendants for the white Pullman car passengers.

Working for the railroad, however, was one of the best jobs a Black man could have in those days. Many Black men who were college graduates worked on the road – as it was called – as dining car waiters, cooks, or porters, and were members of the Union of Sleeping Car Porters. A. Philip Randolph led the union and was instrumental in initiating the Civil Rights Movement after World War II.

The romance of train travel had vanished. There were no more dining cars – which Black folks couldn't use anyway. Porters were gone. Conductors were Black and white. And the railroad cars were dated with well-worn seats. But I was excited. I took the train in the Black customary way, with cold fried chicken wrapped in wax paper in a shoebox with a sliced pound cake. The train no longer stopped in Cairo to segregate the railroad cars before crossing into Kentucky. It was still an overnight ride, but two or three hours shorter.

I got off the train in Birmingham wearing my brand new stingy brim black hat, new finger-tip length raglan sleeve topcoat, new gray flannel Ivy League suit, spread collar white-on-white shirt with a black string tie, new silk pocket square, and new black tasseled loafers. I was sharp and full of myself as I went down the steps from the train platform. And then, suddenly, I stopped.

The train station was a new building. At the foot of the stairs were two doors leading into the station waiting room. Above each door was a large sign in bold, black, block letters. One read "COLORED" and the other read "WHITE."

My ego deflated. I didn't feel special anymore. The signs reminded me that Black people – no matter who or what we became – were still considered inferior to many white people in America.

The waiting room of this building went from the ridiculous to the sublime. It had what appeared to be black leather seating with silver arm rests and legs above a terrazzo floor. Situated in the middle of the room was a long rectangular planter of artificial plants dividing the space in half, one side for white people and one side for people of color (or, as we were known then, "colored people"). There was one ticket counter, but two racially divided sets of male and female restrooms. To further illustrate the illogic of racial separation, there were separate water fountains – one for Blacks and one for whites – next to one elevator for everybody.

I realized the absurdity and basic unfairness of Jim Crow. African Americans in the 1940s lived with the cognitive dissonance of their plight by keeping a positive attitude about themselves as people. That's where my positive self-reinforcement comes from.

Where I once faced legally sanctioned inequality, years later as director of affirmative action I could create state-sponsored equality. These memories deeply influenced my attitude toward my new job.

Creating fairness in the hiring process consisted of changing the traditional closed search process of word-of-mouth for new positions to an open advertising process in which personal alliance building increases opportunities for previously excluded minorities. Traditionally, faculty colleagues talked among themselves about career opportunities – creating an "old boys' network."

Fair employment practices begin with increasing access. In this case, we did so through national advertising for faculty and professional positions. The "affirmative" part of affirmative action is the intentional effort to find and cultivate qualified people of color to apply for positions – regardless of whether they know the right people or not.

It is entirely possible to follow fair hiring procedures and never achieve representative fairness. I maintain that people in any job, at any company or university, always hire people they like – and often that's someone who's like them. If prejudice exists in the process, to be fair there must be a change in how we define who and what we like.

Facing the task of filling a position where the top candidate was a white male from Mississippi, I found my own bigotry. Rather than being fair to him, I rationalized my attitude by making another candidate's personal values more consistent with my own. As in the case of qualified people of color being considered by whites who don't want to hire them, I was inclined to overlook or downplay the Mississippian's fitness for the position because of my knowledge of the history of racial discrimination in the South. However, it was still unfair to penalize this single job applicant.

I confronted my bias against white people from the South, particularly Mississippi, and changed what and who I liked so I could hire the best candidate. I hired the man from Mississippi and found that we had similar cultural touchstones spawned from historic southern origins. Even though I grew up in Chicago many of my cultural values are based on southern traditions, owing to so many Black Americans' southern roots. Though I still have that bias, I work to overcome it in the name of fairness and social justice.

National data illustrated a critical shortage of Black PhDs in all fields. University of Iowa history professor Sidney James was quietly committed to equity and diversity. He called me one day to discuss an unusual graduate application he had gotten from a Black student.

"There's a student in Arkansas who says he's interested in studying the Russian Revolution," Professor James told me. "Although he has a strong record in African American history, it's unusual because he has no background in Russian history. I wonder if this could be a mistake."

With slight bemusement, I listened carefully and wondered how I could tell a professor anything about admitting a doctoral student in his field. I was clearly in over my head. I didn't have a clue about how to approach the problem – except to call and talk to the brother.

"Professor James, if I could talk to him, I might be able to help clarify his intentions," I offered.

Although I didn't know what to do, I surely wasn't going to pass up an opportunity to possibly develop an ally in an outstanding academic department. Professor James agreed. I got the student's telephone number and called him.

"I'm involved in recruiting potential Black scholars for the University of Iowa," I began. "I'm calling because our Department of History may want to admit you to a doctoral program, but it wasn't clear what area you want to research."

His name was R.D. Rucker, and he sounded kind and appreciated the call. I was afraid he might think this was a case of white folks getting a Black person to call to tell him he wasn't qualified. Discrimination delivered from your own stings differently, but still hurts nonetheless.

"I want to use my perspective as an African American historian to study the views of Leon Trotsky as they relate to the formation of Black socialists in the United States," Rucker said confidently.

After our conversation, I called Professor James to share with him my impressions of R.D. Professor James decided to admit R.D. to the doctoral program.

About a year later, R.D. came to my office with a question.

"I'm progressing well in my program, but I need to learn Russian. I've heard about a summer Intensive Russian Language Program at Indiana University that I can take, but I need funds to do it."

The history department didn't have the money, so R.D. was asking me for assistance. I truly believe that when a student is doing his or her best, that I – on behalf of the University – should find a way to help. We never lost a student doing that. Sometimes you had to pad the playing field with funding to level it.

So, I said, as I usually did in similar situations with EOP students, "At this point, I don't have an answer for you, but I follow the adage that where there's a will, there's a way." We got the funds R.D. needed, and he finished his program.

I wanted to use a similar approach to encourage and assist faculty departments to recruit and appoint Black faculty. President Boyd saw to it that I got a small budget to supplement our efforts. Once again, I found myself working with the history department.

They were trying to attract a promising young Black scholar from Princeton University named Jonathan Walton. The department had decided to appoint him before he completed his oral examinations for his PhD.

"We'd really like to get him, but he's concerned about funds to go back to Princeton to finish his exams after his appointment begins," someone in the department told me. The department head said he wished he could help but there was no room in his budget.

"If you can get him, I can commit travel funds for his return to Princeton for one or two trips to finish his work for his degree," I said.

Jonathan came to Iowa and made an outstanding contribution to the Department of History in the study of African American history.

I accommodated students in these situations in part because of my unique reporting responsibilities. I had bifurcated reporting duties for management of the Iowa Memorial Union and Residence Halls to the vice president for administrative services, Shanhouse, and to the vice president for student services, Hubbard. As director of affirmative action, I was responsible for President Boyd's initiatives to foster and monitor the leadership being taken by vice presidents, deans, and department heads to create a more diverse University community – and that meant recruiting quality students, staff, and faculty of color and helping them thrive.

I loved the degrees of freedom I found to create meaningful outcomes for various constituencies. These experiences helped me understand the human elements of complex organizations. Given the eclectic assortment of my administrative responsibilities, I assumed the task of working across the university as a horizontal, rather than a vertical, structure. It became clear to me that to increase institutional equity, I had to learn how people interacted throughout the university. Only then could I work to integrate initiatives for social change with the administration's standard practices.

In 1978 I was given a different set of duties when I was appointed associate dean of students, reporting solely to Dean Philip Hubbard, but affirmative fairness was ingrained in my administrative responsibilities.

Chapter Nine:

The Divestment Movement

S
ocial activism calling for universities to divest the stocks of companies doing business in South Africa, due to its government's practice of apartheid, began in the mid-1970s. Naturally, as a Black man who prided himself on being an advocate for social justice, I emotionally supported the broad purposes of the movement. I faced Jim Crow, which wasn't called "apartheid," but it had plenty in common with it.

The social activism in South Africa followed the lead of demonstrations in the American South. In June 1976, Black children and young adults led an uprising of Black students in Johannesburg's Soweto Township. Children opposed being forced to take instruction in Afrikaans, the language of the country's white minority. Student activism there was an attempt to pressure the South African government to dismantle the racist system of apartheid and to disband the homelands to which many Black South Africans had been banished.

The Rev. Leon H. Sullivan, a Black Baptist minister from Philadelphia and a member of General Motors' board of directors, developed a corporate code of conduct promoting corporate social responsibility. The result was the Sullivan Principles which became the blueprint for ending apartheid. The principles were introduced in 1977 emphasizing nondiscrimination in work facilities, equal and fair employment practices, equal pay for equal or comparable work, initiation and development of training for supervisory and administrative positions, increases in numbers of Black and other nonwhite managers and supervisors, and improvement in quality of life outside of the work environments. In my judgment, this kept the U.S. in the game of active opposition through direct actions.

Iowa law prevented the University from buying or selling stock in the private stock market. All stocks the UI held had been received as gifts, and proceeds were used to fund student financial aid, faculty support, or other services in accordance with the wishes of the donors.

There was consensus among UI administrators that even if the University could conduct a blind sale of a minor amount of stock, it would merely serve as a symbolic protest and wouldn't affect corporate actions on the issues. On the other hand, the University could be more effective from within the system through the exercise of proxy voting. In this position, the UI stood a better chance of influencing corporate conduct and best safeguard the integrity of investments.

Led by President Sandy Boyd – and consistent with the policy of upholding and promoting human rights and acting financially responsible as a state institution – the University of Iowa administration took a position to vote shareholder resolutions opposing apartheid. Social activists didn't agree. They wanted complete withdrawal from doing business in South Africa until apartheid was abolished.

I experienced direct action demonstrations against F.W. Woolworth in Chicago in 1960 protesting segregated lunch counters in Woolworth stores in the South. These were symbolic actions too. Through the years, I came to see that symbolic actions could have significant impact when applied persistently. Based on that belief, I felt sanguine that in the long run voting shareholder resolutions would have a changing effect to create economic and social justice in South Africa.

As a means of social protest, President Boyd tasked me and his assistant Casey Mahon to attend various shareholder meetings to vote in favor of social responsibility resolutions. My first exposure to the corporate world came at the annual shareholder meeting of the Mobil Oil Corporation (before its merger with Exxon). The meeting took place in the palatial Crowne Plaza Hotel at Country Club Plaza in Kansas City, Missouri. I stayed at the hotel the night before the meeting.

On the top floor of the hotel was an elegantly appointed restaurant and lounge. After checking into my hotel room late in the evening, I went up to the lounge to have a drink and relax after my day of travel. As I settled into a comfortable leather chair, I noticed sounds coming from a set of tables on a platform area in the center of the room.

Seated in a cluster were a half dozen fashionably dressed, middle-aged, tanned, salt-and-pepper haired men engaged in casual conversation, surrounded by a haze of aromatic cigar smoke. As I studied my surroundings, I realized I was the only Black person in the room. While I had long since adjusted to being sensitive about being the only and lonely Black person in a setting, this seemed different because of what had drawn my attention to the group. I had a curious inclination about the group that kept me riveted. I imagined they were corporate executives of Mobil Oil. I had assigned celebrity status and the presumption of white superiority to them.

My first celebrity experience was when I was ten years old and chanced to meet Bobby Avila, the star second baseman for the Cleveland Indians, in the 1950s. After a day game against the Chicago White Sox, I was hanging out around the team's ballpark three blocks from my house with other boys near the visiting team's locker room exit. After each game, there was always a chartered bus waiting to take the ballplayers downtown to their hotel. The bus had already left by the time a player exited the visiting team's locker room. He didn't have a car, and there wasn't a taxi around.

He was a slightly built, muscular, average height, bronze-complexioned Latino with straight black hair neatly combed into a puffed style. We recognized him right away.

"Hey, any you guys know how to get downtown?" Avila asked us in his Spanish accent.

"I do," I piped up. "You have to take the streetcar."

Like the Pied Piper with us kids alongside and trailing behind, Avila started toward the streetcar stop. As we walked, I couldn't take my eyes off him. He was a non-white Major League player in the early 1950s, so he had to have superior ability. I thought, "He's a normal person – just like other guys I know." But I presumed his superiority as a person based on his status as a big-league ballplayer.

Observing the group of corporate executives, I presumed their superiority too, but it was based on the precept of white superiority and Black inferiority I internalized through dual conscious cultural experiences. I didn't realize it at the time, but I was reacting to the cultural mythology entrenched through centuries of oppression African Americans were forced to endure. While I associated celebrity and higher status with both the Mobil executives and Bobby Avila, I identified with the ballplayer in a way I couldn't fathom with the corporate executives.

With the baseball player, I was in a comfortable environment and on familiar ground – my neighborhood. With the Mobil Oil executives, I was in a formal, luxury, and highly impersonal environment. Because of what I call the Jackie Robinson syndrome, I believed I could aspire to be like Bobby Avila. The executives looked like normal people, but in my mind, they were better than people of color because these men ran a multinational corporation that strongly influenced the lives of millions of Black people in South Africa and around the world.

My discomfort in the hotel lounge might reasonably be attributed to the lack of exposure I, and many others like me, experience in everyday life to negate the precepts of white superiority and Black inferiority in business and social interactions that affect our self-concepts.

Under President James Freedman the University of Iowa continued to vote for shareholder resolutions that increased corporate social responsibility in South

Africa. In October 1984, the student government passed a resolution recommending that the University sell its shares in companies doing business in South Africa.

In his annual speech to the faculty, President Freedman said, "One of the most effective ways a university can meet social responsibility is to redouble its efforts in doing what it does best: to provide education of the highest quality and to make it broadly accessible. To that end, the University of Iowa has initiated the South African Scholarship Program (SASP), a determined effort to increase the number of Black students from South Africa who study at the University."

"This program will not change the face of South Africa in the short run, but it is a start toward preserving the vocabulary of hope in the precincts of apartheid," he concluded prophetically.

A proposal to create a scholarship program for Black Southern Africans had its genesis during a conversation with the forward-thinking director of the Office of International Education and Services (OIES), Dr. Steven Arum. Steve was an assertive internationalist and advocate for global human rights. The sponsoring organization wanted to know if our University would be willing to provide partial support for Black South African students International Institute for Educational Planning - UNESCO (IIEP) identified and recruited. President Freedman made the decision to support the students with the amounts equivalent to stock proceeds from companies doing business in South Africa. Referrals came from IIEP and other international referral agencies connected to South Africa. The students encouraged us to use the descriptor "Southern Africa" for the program because many of them were living in exile in various countries within that region. The first group of twelve students – three undergraduates and nine graduates – enrolled in fall, 1984. At the initiation of the program President Freedman sent me a note;

Dear Phil,

I am very pleased by the success of the South African Scholarship Program and deeply grateful to you for helping to make it possible. When we began last December, I did not dare dream that we would have twelve Black students from South Africa enrolled this fall. I congratulate you for making it happen. And I send you my warmest appreciation.

Sincerely,
James O. Freedman,

President

In the second year of the program, eight new students – five undergraduates, two graduates, and one in intensive English – enrolled and received University support. Seven new students arrived in the third year of the program – 1986-1987. SASP tuition scholarships were the primary source of support, and one student was a Fulbright Scholar.

By the end of 1987 all the graduate students – except one, who transferred – earned master's degrees. Four went back to South Africa, and one went to Zambia. The other four remained to work on doctoral degrees in biochemistry, education, and journalism.

Throughout the existence of the SASP during the 1980s and early 1990s, the participants were strong and dedicated to bringing about nonviolent revolution through improving the educational and economic conditions of Black people throughout Southern Africa. Even though many of the students experienced personal, economic and cultural adjustment challenges, they persevered.

****

Student opinions about divestiture ranged from the modest positions to activists' zealous calls for full divestiture. A national day of solidarity to protest racial policies in South Africa was held on more than two dozen campuses – including the University of Iowa's – on April 24, 1985. It was a warm, sunny Thursday three weeks before the end of the semester. On the Pentacrest lawn, at the center of the campus, students lounged while others strolled between classes on the sidewalks connecting Schaeffer and MacBride Halls. Leaves began to form on the large oak and ash trees, casting midday shadows.

A modest crowd formed on the lawn. The atmosphere was a mixture of nonchalance among the sunbathers, furrowed-brow intensity among protestors clustered around a platform, and curiosity among those lurking on the fringe of the gathering. Speakers assembled in front of a handmade banner reading "No business in South Africa." The crowd grew as it lured in casual observers, curious passers, and dedicated activists until it numbered more than a hundred.

Among the speakers was a SASP South African student named Moyisi Majeke. I knew from our many conversations that his position amounted to, "You can never trust the Boers," meaning the white Dutch South Africans. He opposed President Reagan's policy of constructive engagement that reduced pressure on the South African government to change. Instead, Majeke wanted the U.S. to take decisive action against South Africa, tantamount to withdrawal of economic cooperation with the country's government, while at the same time providing political and economic aid to the African National Congress (ANC) – which eventually toppled the apartheid government in South Africa. He wanted to have it both ways – divestiture and intensification of engagement.

A student organization, the Iowa Coalition Against Apartheid, sponsored the rally. In rapid succession, without introductions, speakers voiced their views – varied passionate laments about the conditions of apartheid and criticisms of U.S. businesses and universities for contributing to the South African government's oppressive policies. The campus movement didn't resonate highly among African American students so most of the speakers were white students. The final speaker took the microphone with a burst of energy, clapping his hands, waving his arms, moving back and forth across the platform to get the crowd excited to repeat a chant, "No business, no business, no business in South Africa."

Local television reporters, with video and still photo cameras, swarmed the fringe of the gathering, focusing on the hive of students that appeared to grow in proportion to the media attention. When it appeared that a critical mass had formed, with gyrating arms and clenched fists pumping, the speakers descended from the stage as the leader with the microphone said, "Let's give the president our demands."

This was a new experience for the Jim Freedman presidency. The Administrative Liaison Group (ALG) was in a lull since the late '70s, when the last wave of campus demonstrations – against the Vietnam War and CIA – crested. My role had changed. I was the nominal head of the ALG although I still considered myself – as I had in Flint and at the Lower North Center in Chicago's Cabrini-Green Homes – a foot soldier at the scenes of controversial events. I was outside among the crowd. My objective was to jawbone with demonstrators in attempts to avoid or minimize confrontation between them and the administration or law enforcement.

I entered the first-floor office at the south end of Jessup Hall as the crowd began to move toward Jessup Hall. Two public safety officers were posted inside the president's office. I gazed through the glass panes of the room's French doors and recognized the faces of the activists leading a growing collection of onlookers. They streamed up the first flight of stairs immediately to the right of the door to Room 101 at the south end of the corridor. The press followed, planting themselves on the landing between the first and second floor staircases.

Peering through the glass panes from outside the office double doors were six seemingly unsure but determined coalition leaders – four men and two women. Directly in their sightline were the two security officers, a receptionist seated at her desk, Ann Huntzinger and Mary Lynn Grant – two of Freedman's administrative assistants – and me. A six-foot tall, lightly bearded young man held in his left hand a typed document, while his right hand pushed down on the door handle to open it. In military fashion, his five fellow demonstrators followed single file into the room. The man with the printed demands, the de facto leader of the group, approached the receptionist's desk about twenty feet inside the door.

In a low monotone, with reporters looking on and cameras rolling, the young man carrying the petition said to the receptionist, "We're here to present our list of demands to President Freedman for the University of Iowa to join other leading universities in opposing the oppressive apartheid policies in South Africa. We demand that the University of Iowa divest immediately."

The activists body language telegraphed their low expectations.

Then, Julia Mears, who succeeded Casey Mahon as an assistant to President Freedman, came in from a side office in Room 101. Julia, an intellectual and committed progressive activist since the '60s, had a gift for blending the serious and the humorous.

"President Freedman isn't here right now, but I can take your petition and be sure that he gets it as soon as he returns," she said, disarming the delegation.

"We demand more than handing him a piece of paper," said a Black woman, the only student of color in the group. "The University has been stalling too long. We demand action now. No business in South Africa!"

Anticipating that further conversation would only elevate tensions, Julia suggested, "Why don't we step into the conference room so you can let us hear your position more fully for the president to respond to?"

By this time, a group of about twenty adolescent undergraduates, predominantly white and male, had crowded inside the doors to the office. The sextet in the leading delegation looked at each other quizzically, as though they were trying to reach instant wordless consensus. They struck a cool pose of pseudo self-assurance as they sauntered into the dim conference room. Like lemmings, the students filtered into the room. There were twice as many demonstrators and reporters than there were chairs.

It was about 3 o'clock in the afternoon. Being veterans of this kind of thing, Julia and I positioned ourselves with our backs to the door. The polemics began as soon as we closed the door. During an hour, practically every person in the room, except the reporters, had something to say; and each time it quickly escalated to self-motivated militancy, based more on emotion than on logic and fact. Julia and I borrowed Muhammad Ali's rope-a-dope approach. We knew if we didn't become defensive, they might soon tire of their own ranting.

After ninety minutes I tried to end the session.

"We appreciate your concerns, and I personally admire your commitment to equal rights not only in this country and in South Africa but around the world," I said as Julia nodded in agreement.

"We will definitely convey to the president the seriousness of your demands," Julia followed.

The mood in the room had become more relaxed as though all sides were reaching closure to the meeting. That lasted for moments until a charismatic guy in sunglasses rose from his seat in the corner.

"The University needs to meet our demand to divest all stocks held in companies doing business in South Africa immediately," he shouted while gesturing dramatically. "The time is now for no business in South Africa. We're going to sit in until President Freedman complies with our demands."

Julia and I had the same reaction. Wordlessly, we turned and left the room. Standing, looking at the door quizzically, were the president's assistants Mary Lynn Grant and Ann Huntzinger, who whispered their confusion.

"With the office being open now, technically they're not disrupting any function of the University," Julia explained with an attorney-like air of calm certainty. "So long as they stay in the conference room, we have a little time to figure out a reasonable, and hopefully, peaceful response. Let's get on the phone to Mr. Freedman to bring him up to speed on what's happening and see if he can get the vice presidents together to tell us what direction we might go in."

The security officers left for a shift change, and Ann and Mary Lynn went home. About a half-hour after the office closed, President Freedman called back. Julia took the call. He directed us not to take any law enforcement action for the time being.

He also told us to monitor the situation and keep him informed. We'd already decided to keep the security officers in place for as long as the sit-in continued.

Based on my experiences to maintain reasonable time, place, and manner in previous demonstrations, I said, "I think we should keep the outer doors to the office locked. If someone wants to leave the conference room, they must leave the office and the building, with no re-entry since everything is closed for the night."

Julia smiled and said in her chuckling, sarcastic manner, "You mean no bathroom breaks?"

We got back in touch with the president to tell him our plan, and he had no objections.

My pulse quickened, and perspiration trickled down my back as I went back into the conference room. I wasn't convinced the students were prepared to accept the consequences of their actions. Even though I felt they were uninformed, I was conflicted about opposing the sit-in. Without civil disobedience, there would have been no modern Civil Rights Movement. On one hand, I was proud to see young people engaged in dissent against racial oppression. On the other hand, I didn't want to disrespect the moral principle of civil disobedience by patronizing the dissenters.

I laid out the conditions we would allow for their demonstration.

"Since you've decided to exercise your right to dissent by occupying this office, you may exercise that right within the bounds of reasonable time, place, and manner without curtailing the functions of the University," I began, as the protestors listened quietly. "However, when University functions resume in this office in the morning, we will have to ask you to leave this conference room. In the meantime, anyone may leave this office and the building at any time. Other offices in this complex are closed, so for security reasons they are off limits. When you decide to leave this room, you will be escorted out of the building."

I tried to empathize with the students. Strategically, it was important to respect their dissent while at the same time affirming the University's commitment to human rights – thus humanizing the bureaucracy – by opposing apartheid through the most effective administrative mechanism available at that time. To do that, it was necessary to hold the demonstrators responsible for their actions if they violated University policy or the law.

It was clear to me that we were in for the long haul, so I decided to stay in the office along with campus security through the night. Julia came in early the next morning.

As the night wore on, some of the students trickled out of the conference room and left the building. Shortly after midnight, between twelve and fifteen activists remained. It occurred to me to request that campus security patrol the outside under the windows to the conference room, in case the protesters tried to get assistance from the outside.

I spent the night half-sitting and half-lying between two office chairs in a small room adjacent to the president's office. From time to time, I dozed for a brief nap but spent most of the night trying to figure out how to end peacefully the sit-in in the morning. The two officers sat in chairs and slept outside the conference room door. Conversation inside the room was continuous until the reporter left at about 1 a.m.

My stomach and back and neck muscles were tight from being perched on two chairs overnight. In the morning sun, the campus had a serene quality that belied the dissent within Jessup Hall. In anticipation of how things might end, I thought it would be beneficial to begin attempting to end the sit-in as early as possible and avoid a major confrontation. At first light, I phoned Julia at home.

"By mid-morning, there will be a lot fewer protesters in the conference room than we started with last night," I told her. "I think we might suggest to President Freedman to begin the process early in the morning to allow the office to open for business at 8 a.m."

Having experienced protests, she understood the significance of limiting publicity; a demonstration might be fueled by additional participants who just happened to show up shortly after the television cameras. I hadn't heard back from Julia by the time the staff in the president's office came to work. My stomach was in knots – more from an adrenaline rush than from not having eaten in almost twenty-four hours.

I was afraid of the unknown, and I anticipated the worst that could happen. What would President Freedman decide? When would I know it?

I hoped he realized that, if we didn't act soon, conditions could encourage protests outside of the president's office in support of those in the conference room.

We waited throughout the morning for some word back from the president about our next steps. There was a renewal of activity as reporters with cameras began to appear outside the office. We kept the doors locked.

I was fidgety and anxious. Even though my insides were raging, outwardly I tried to maintain a calm demeanor. I learned from previous protests that we needed to clear the office of protesters while the group was manageable, rather than let a crowd of protesters gather.

As I suspected, by noon, students began to swarm in front of the TV cameras outside the door to the office. Within a half hour, bodies lined the hall from wall to wall and the whole length of the space, sitting and blocking the staircases and the doors to other offices. We had reached the point of no return.

The president would have to act to restore the University's ability to function. He received word that the sit-in on the first floor had effectively shut down Jessup Hall for classes and University operations.

President Freedman called the protesters in the conference room to get them to accept the UI's stance to oppose apartheid through corporate shareholder resolutions. After much discussion, they affirmed their dissent. President Freedman decided we should end the demonstration by clearing the conference room and the hallways of protesters. When they refused to leave, we called law enforcement to remove the activists.

A platoon of uniformed but unarmed officers – they didn't even have handcuffs or wear headgear – filed onto the first floor wearing rubber gloves. The press reported that although all the students went peacefully, most of the 140 students refused to stand and had to be carried out of the building. They were taken by bus to the University Police station, charged with trespassing, and released.

The actions of these activists and their peers on other campuses – both before and on the national day of solidarity – had a significant effect on universities, corporations, and governments. Eventually, President Freedman appointed a committee to review the economic viability of all University of Iowa shareholdings in U.S. companies conducting business in South Africa. The Iowa Legislature created and passed legislation permitting the University to sell shares in the stock market.

 Direct actions by Black South Africans, the changing social norms in the country, and international pressures led to the election of Nelson R. Mandela as the first Black president in post-apartheid South Africa in 1999.

President Freedman continued the University's commitment to human rights. I was pleased to receive a personal note from him after the student demonstrations.

Dear Phil,

I write to express my gratitude for the selfless contribution you have made during the last two weeks. I truly do not know what the university would have done without your good sense and dedication. You have my deepest appreciation.

Jim

Chapter Ten:

Diverging Paths

Historically, Black students weren't barred from entering the Iowa Memorial Union, but they were excluded from programs at the IMU. A story I heard from University of Iowa alumnus Byron Burford, a native Mississippian and professor in Iowa's art school, illustrated the diverging social paths.

"When I was a graduate student at Iowa, the Duke Ellington Orchestra played a campus dance in the union's Main Lounge in 1939," Burford recalled. "Black students couldn't go on the dance floor. They had to stand behind ropes around the edge of the ballroom."

When I began oversight of the IMU, I took a tour of the 100,000-square foot facility. I was astounded by the building's complexity and the difficulty of going from the original building to added pavilions.

My challenge was to change the atmosphere, increase staff morale, and create a new sense of campus tradition – one that included contributions of Black, other non-white, and international students. I'd witnessed the link between administrative and socio-cultural outcomes, and it inspired me to create pathways for social change by broadening the diversity of cultural participation at the IMU.

The University of Iowa Hospital and Clinics has a labyrinth of passageways through multiple buildings. I asked the hospital architect Gene Anderson to go on a walking tour through the IMU to give me some hints about how to help visitors find their way through the IMU.

"From an architectural point of view, it really needs attention," said Gene, who was also an accomplished artist and sculptor. "It may not be possible to make a clear and simple set of directions in a minimum number of signs to get from one place to another in this building. It needs to have a series of bridging pathways across the open patio space, and from one section to another above the first floor."

I used Gene's insightful pathway analogy as a symbolic and foundation basis to create continuity to improve the functional and financial aspects of the IMU, while restoring its vitality as an integrated student life center.

The process of securing funding for a major renovation was a new experience for me. In 1982, I received initial presidential approval for my proposal to finance a $10.5 million renovation plan of the IMU.

I was ambivalent about stepping into the entirely new realm of university-wide responsibility. Ten million dollars was more money than I had ever imagined – much less thought of managing.

I quickly realized that dreams cost money. That didn't seem evident to others with different priorities during the planning process. With this project, I realized I was accountable for more than equity program development and management. I had to meld together the wishes and diverging interests as part of my broader administrative responsibility.

The IMU is a memorial dedicated to men and women who served in America's military. There's a marble plaque in the entrance of the 1927 addition to the IMU that reads: "And if this magnificent structure is to fulfill the dream out of which it has arisen, it can only do so by stirring the impulses of the young men and women of Iowa to lives of service to mankind."

The University of Iowa's mandate is to serve the people of the state of Iowa – as well as achieving national goals of access and equity. Historically, the unique role of the IMU did not include a requirement to ensure building access for people in wheelchairs. As a result, none of the main entrances to the building were wheelchair accessible. Direct access by wheelchair was only available through a ground-floor entrance on the north side of the building. Federal mandates in the 1960s required the renovation to include reasonable accommodations for people with disabilities, including visual impairments.

For students, faculty, and staff to continue having free access to meeting rooms, we needed to generate more revenue to support the IMU's operations. Opening a bookstore provided a solid source of income to maintain access to the free services the campus provided through the union.

As initiator, I had a prerogative to create new proposals for the project. However, in a system where modicums of power represent differing paths taken and not taken based on areas of expertise and involvement, consensus is essential. In this organizational construct, direction was determined through consensus of the most common paths for diverging interests.

During initial project planning in 1980, I got a fortuitous phone call from McKinley "Deacon" Davis, one of the originators of the University of Iowa Black Alumni Association. In 1951, Deacon was among the first Black students offered a full-ride basketball scholarship in the Big Ten Conference – and the first at Iowa.

Deacon proposed the University of Iowa establish a hall of honor in tribute to Black pioneers who provided extraordinary service to Black students and the Iowa City community during segregated times and to recognize the outstanding achievements of Black student athletes during that era. The proposal acknowledged the divergent pathways of racial segregation with societal efforts toward reconciliation, diversity and inclusion.

"I think it's a great idea," I said. "I'll run it by President Boyd and Vice President Hubbard to see what they think." They both thought the idea had great merit for acknowledging our past and recognizing the strides Iowa City and the University had made in expanding human rights. The Black Alumni Hall of Honor was designated for the new addition.

The Iowa Black Alumni Association selected the initial honorees: Estella Louise Ferguson, Helen Lemme, Emlen "the Gremlin" Lewis Tunnell and Frederick "Duke" Slater.

Ferguson, or "Mother Ferg," as she was called by Black students, established and operated a rooming house for Black male students – who, as did their Black female peers, faced housing discrimination from the University and local landlords – until 1947.

Helen Lemme was a University of Iowa graduate and a member of the historically Black Delta Sigma Theta Sorority at Iowa. She worked as a laboratory assistant at the University of Iowa Hospitals and Clinics. The basement recreation room of the Iowa City house she shared with her husband Allyn was a quasi-student center for many Black students when the IMU wasn't a comfortable gathering place for them. Annually during homecoming, it was a tradition for former students to party at the Lemmes' home and autograph one of the basement walls. The night before she died in a house fire on December 15, 1968, Mrs. Lemme had hosted a party for Iowa's first group of EOP students.

Emlen "the Gremlin" Tunnell was the first Black player drafted by the New York Football Giants and later became the first Black assistant coach in the history of the National Football League (NFL). The former Iowa football star is also a member of the Pro Football Hall of Fame.

Frederick "Duke" Slater is the first Black All-American in Iowa football history and is regarded as one of the program's greatest linemen. After graduating from Iowa, he played 10 years of professional football, including two seasons as the only Black player in the NFL. Slater went to law school at Iowa in the off-season and earned his law degree in 1928. After retiring from football, he moved to Chicago and became an assistant district attorney. He was elected as a municipal court judge in 1948 and served as a judge in Cook County for almost two decades before his death in 1966.

It's significant that those initial honorees in the Black Alumni Hall of Honor were athletes and providers of housing – athletics and communal living are cornerstones of the college experience. Black students found solace inside the veil in places like the Lemmes' basement, or self-prescribed enclaves in the Iowa Memorial Union. Social lives and dating were limited for the Black student-athletes because there were fewer Black women on campus and dating white women was socially unacceptable.

Black students weren't always welcome at Iowa, but they persevered and created a community for themselves – making fond memories and taking great pride in their time at the University. That was the rationale for recognition; honoring those who provided supportive services that made living in the University community possible as well as those who overcame great odds to accomplish their quests for excellence in life and to be of service to mankind. Harold Bradley, who painted the portraits for the Black Alumni Hall of Honor, played football at the University of Iowa and graduated with a degree in art in the 1950s.

This IMU renovation project, completed in 1988, linked the 1920s and 1965 pavilions with a two-story atrium on the second and third floors, while creating a terrace lobby entrance. The Black Alumni Hall of Honor occupied a wall near that atrium. President Hunter Rawlings recognized the Iowa Black Alumni Hall of Honor during an opening celebration of the new addition, which also commemorated the IMU's 65th anniversary.

In the November 1989 issue of American Schools and University Facility Planning, the IMU renovation was cited as one of six outstanding union projects of that period.

****

Du Bois' concept of dual consciousness represents a sensation of divided identity among African Americans. In one sense, Black students felt the Civil Rights Movement and student demands on predominantly white campuses increased opportunities to advance diversity on campus. In another sense, they felt they didn't fully belong within the social, academic, and historic culture of the university. Dual consciousness illustrates the dilemma of diverging pathways in broadening the concept of diversity and cultural inclusion in campus life and programs.

To recognize African American culture, Black students demanded recognition in the curriculum, more Black faculty and administrators, and more Black students in 1967. They formed a Black Student Union to petition the University administration to create a center for Black students to express their social and cultural identity on campus.

As the new Black administrator, I worked with the students to establish the first African-American Cultural Center (AACC) on campus in 1968. It was in a frame house on the corner of Capitol and Market Streets. In 1971 the "Afro House" (as it came to be called) was relocated to a larger house at the corner of Market and Madison Streets across from the IMU. The first Afro center became the location for the first women's center in 1971.

Three students – two Latinos and one Native American, Anthony "Tony" Zavala, Nancy "Rusty" Barceló, and Ruth Pushetonequa – organized the Chicano and American Indian Student organization. In 1971, they proposed to share the house of the Office of International Programs on Clinton Street between Jefferson and Market Streets. In 1973 the Latino, Native American Cultural Center (LNACC) was opened on Melrose Avenue across from the College of Law.

The Afro House was moved a second time in 1976 to a house with more useable programing space. It was located across the Iowa River north of Hillcrest Residence Hall (on what was Byington Street) near the bridge over Riverside Drive. The house was actively used for artistic and cultural programs and social dances. The foundation of the house became compromised and had to be vacated and torn down. The AACC was relocated a third time to the location on Melrose Avenue across the street from the LNACC and adjacent to the College of Law.

In 1998 I initiated a plan to improve the infrastructure of student services. Concurrent with a plan for an athletic department learning center, I initiated a plan for a new west campus residence hall. I was resolute that future campus planning should include the cultural center concept. In conjunction with the new hall, I proposed to create a new multicultural center within a "union-west" concept within the new hall.

I had mixed emotions about the physical conditions of the AACC and LNACC. My sense of dual consciousness reminded me of a childhood admonition always to do the best you can with whatever you have no matter how simple. I grew up in a community with few physical advantages – probably like where many EOP students came from. In our communities, people took pride in what they had and made the most of what they could afford. I worried about how some perceptions of white superiority might become the basis for reinforcing negative beliefs of Black and brown students based on the appearances of the centers in comparison to other campus buildings.

I realized I was opening myself to a great deal of criticism from minority students when I opened a conversation about developing a new concept of multicultural center housing. I proposed the University construct a permanent multicultural facility consistent with the cultural center interior designs of the two ethnic centers on campus.

Dual consciousness impressions among Black students was that the University was planning to close the cultural centers. While at the same time the University administration considered the centers a focus on inclusions for previously excluded groups. Misinformation caused fear and mistrust in the minority student community. I talked to students to try to build an understanding and support for my proposal.

The controversy took place in a transparent atmosphere. There was constant press coverage from 1998 through the spring of 2000. In February 1999, I met with students at the Afro House to listen to students and describe my concept for future development of the cultural centers. I emphasized that there were no plans to close either of the cultural centers! Few were persuaded by my emotional plea.

A student eloquently expressed the essence of Albert Murrays' concept of the blues idiom when he said, "If we're comfortable here, why do we have to move?" His feelings were consistent with a view many of us learned to live with that "it's not much to look at, and nothing to see, but it's home to me." The blues idiom expresses a primary concern to make life as significant as possible regardless of the circumstances.

In the final analysis, the cost of creating and financing the union west/cultural center project was greater than could be done in conjunction with financing the residence hall proposal. In 2015, a five-hundred-bed residence hall was approved for construction on the east campus and in 2016 named Elizabeth Catlett Residence Hall.

Consistent with Black student perceptions of advances in diversity without comparable feelings of cultural inclusion, other culturally marginalized groups sought to create paths for cultural inclusion through established cultural centers within the campus community.

As interim president in 2003, Willard "Sandy" Boyd concurred with the request of Asian students for a cultural center. I worked with the students to develop the Asian

Pacific American Cultural Center in a frame house located on the west campus adjacent to the health sciences campus on Melrose Avenue. In 2006 in recognition of broadening social norms, I worked with President David Skorton to establish the Lesbian, Gay, Bisexual, Transgender Center.

Chapter Eleven:

Hustler for **Social Change**

reating social change through organization development is like being an institutional gadfly through deliberate interference of the status quo in an amiable way. I tried to be a catalyst for change through my administrative responsibilities. I considered my charge to find or, if necessary, create opportunities to enhance the quality of campus life. In terms of equity issues, I found ways to make the specific become the general, only to later discover that some white students often shared similar struggles to those of their EOP peers.

In the mid-to-late '80s, when Leslie Sims was dean of the Graduate College, I proposed an idea like what we had done with the law school: transfer existing university administrative funds to the college to create a full-time EOP recruitment and admissions position.

Dean Sims wanted to formalize coordination of minority graduate student recruitment and advising within the Graduate College, and to replace the fragmented approaches that had evolved over the years among departments, Special Support Services (SSS) and the college. Two SSS staff members were responsible for coordinating minority graduate student recruitment. In exchange for the Graduate College creating an office, I arranged to transfer two extremely capable and dedicated administrators, Joseph Henry and Diana Bryant, from SSS to the college. They raised the visibility of the program significantly with a lasting impact on University of Iowa participation in CIC graduate programs for increasing the number of doctoral students of color.

I maintained a relationship with the UI College of Medicine since my early days on campus. Woodrow Morris, a psychologist, served medical students through the dean's office for what might nominally be called "student affairs" for students in the medical college before EOP was created. Students of color admitted through EOP began their enrollment during an intensive summer program, supported in part by Roy J. Carver funds, that allowed the students to acclimate to Iowa and to earn credit in one basic sciences course to lighten their first-year academic load.

Over time, the college changed many practices associated with student life, and eventually the EOP summer program became an option for some white students as well. The advent of federal health professions federal grants and financial aid loan programs was a significant turning point in many regards because there were more students of all backgrounds who had never been able to afford graduate school in medicine or any other health profession.

Students who face institutional adversity – learners of color, LGBT students, those with disabilities or who come from poverty (keeping in mind those groups aren't exclusive) – often need additional support when they begin medical school. Medical faculty and staff realized the need for academic support was growing for all. Teaching methodology had to evolve to address the massive amounts of cognitively complex material in a new curriculum.

Dr. George Baker, a highly sensitive and perceptive pediatrician, was appointed associate dean to create what is now the College of Medicine's Office of Student Affairs and Curriculum. George developed the first learning assistance laboratory in the college. I conferred with him on several occasions as he wrote the federal grant proposal to establish the learning lab. The systematic academic support program invented to level the field for minority students became institutionalized for all students.

After receiving funding through the first Roy J. Carver gift to the University of Iowa – which included funds to support equity initiatives – the law school established a summer program to enhance entering EOP students' writing skills. Professor James Alan McPherson Jr. – the first Black author to win the Pulitzer Prize for fiction, and a graduate of Harvard Law School – led the first summer writing program. The faculty felt the program was so successful that they incorporated it into the school's curriculum for all students.

By the last decade of the 20th century, there was a different mood in the country about equity and affirmative fairness. I sensed the change everywhere; in Iowa City, among my student affairs colleagues in the CIC and from my involvement in national associations.

The greatest barrier to higher education is financial, regardless of race. In the era of Civil Rights legislation during the '60s, President Lyndon B. Johnson proposed and Congress passed the Federal Guaranteed Student Loan program as part of the Higher Education Act of 1965. In 1988 the program was renamed the Robert T. Stafford Loan program, in honor of the Republican U.S. Senator from Vermont who was an advocate for higher education.

My involvement with the National Association of State Universities and Land-

Grant Colleges (NASULGC) – now known as the Association of Public and Land-Grant Universities (APLU) – began in December 1979, and my first assignment was to the Committee on Equal Opportunity. After it was reorganized within the association, the committee became the Commission on Human Resources and Social Change (now the Commission on Access, Diversity and Excellence) – and I served on the executive committee for several years. As chair of a subcommittee on financial aid, I had a unique opportunity to seek ways to emphasize access and equity for underserved students.

Such was the case beginning in the mid-'80s when Thomas A. "Tom" Butts, an expert in financial aid, was responsible for federal relations for the University of Michigan. Tom was Michigan's financial aid director from 1971 to 1977, before spending four years as policy advisor and deputy assistant secretary for student financial assistance for the federal government. He began discussions to replace the Federal Guaranteed Student Loan program with direct loans to students.

As chair of the Student Affairs Task Force on Financial Aid, I worked with the Association's Federal Student Financial Assistance Subcommittee on preparing draft recommendations for the financial assistance section of the reauthorization of the Higher Education Act in 1992. The subcommittee emphasized that "student financial aid should be regarded as a national investment to enhance the development of an intelligent, capable, and diverse workforce and citizenry for the United States in the 21st Century."

The subcommittee noted that by the turn of the 21st century, one-third of the nation's workforce would consist of people of color "and others traditionally underrepresented in higher education. A disproportionate amount of these students come from lower income families." A quarter-century later, our inferences were proven correct.

Though controversial, because it challenged bank lending programs for students, Tom Butts' proposal gained traction among higher education associations, national leaders, congressional staffers as well as a few legislators. Ironically, there didn't seem to be much pushback from the banking community in Washington, D.C., during the first two years leading up to the reauthorization in 1992.

When it seemed as if there might be some real interest among leaders of the capital's higher education associations, the American Council on Education (ACE) – an umbrella leadership group of higher-education presidents – formed a national task force of diverse interests representing private and public two- and four-year colleges and universities and national associations. Through my role with NASULGC, I was asked to join the task force.

The president of the University of Michigan at that time, James "Jim" Duderstadt, was appointed to chair the ACE task force on creating a proposal to replace the bank guaranteed loan program with a direct student loan program from the federal government. Jim's role wasn't enviable because of its high degree of difficulty. Many stakeholders were involved: various higher education institutions, governing boards, and financial institutions affiliated with private and public schools that participated and gained financially from the guaranteed loan program.

An engineer by profession and a humanist by temperament, Jim opened the discussion by trying to ease the group's concerns about the potential politics of creating a complicated legislative proposal. Conversations among committee members from diverse institutions and organizations revealed varying levels of understanding and agreement with Butts' concept.

Using his own vernacular, Duderstadt masterfully reassured the group.

"We're going to take one step at a time, and when we come to a snake in the grass, we'll go back and find a way around it until we find our way through this process," he said.

Congress passed a version of the Direct Loan Program in the final year of the George H.W. Bush administration; however, the president promised to veto it.

The banking lobby put on a full-court press to defeat the direct loan legislation but fell short and had to settle for a compromise: colleges would have the option of staying with the private bank guaranteed loan program or switching to an institutionally based program for direct loans to students. Newly elected President Bill Clinton signed off on that version of the program early in 1993.

Chapter Twelve:

November First

Enhancing the quality of campus life is the essence of social change. A significant goal of student services is to create a safe and healthful environment. Doing so has occasionally meant confronting potential and actual violent protests and deadly events on campus. Over the years, I learned to live with the anxiety of confronting conflicting points of view while working in coordination with law enforcement. On more than one occasion, I've had some concern for my personal safety, but I never actually felt the fear of death like I did on the evening of November 1, 1991.

It was a somber day after a cold and rainy Halloween night; and the forecast for Friday, the first day of November was for colder temperatures with rain, snow, and high winds across the state. The atmosphere was quiet among administrative offices in Jessup Hall. President Rawlings was out of town in Columbus, Ohio, at Ohio State University for a nationally televised football game between Ohio State and Iowa and, newly appointed, vice president (provost) Peter Nathan was also out of town on University business.

Susan Phillips, vice president for finance; Ann Rhodes, vice president for university relations; Julia Mears, assistant to the president; Ann Huntzinger, executive assistant to the president; Mary Lynn Grant, presidential assistant; and office support staff were in the president's office, Room 101 of Jessup Hall. Ann Rhodes, Ann Huntzinger, and Julia Mears regularly participated with me in coordinating campus responses to conflicts on campus through the ALG (administrative liaison group). For more than two decades, I had had an active role in the ALG to maintain a calm, safe, and civil environment on campus.

In the middle of the afternoon, as I sat in my office staring at increasingly adverse weather conditions, anticipating a wet and snowy drive home in the next few hours, I heard a loud commotion in the corridor outside my office on the first floor of Jessup Hall. All at once, with a serious, sober, and dramatic facial expression – my staff colleague Belinda Marner, came through the open doorway to my office and in a voice barely audible above a whisper, said, "The Iowa City Police are in the hall with their guns drawn. Something has happened in academic affairs!" Room 111,

Academic Affairs – the provost's office – is located at the north end of the first-floor corridor adjacent to the north entrance and stairway into Jessup Hall.

My stomach churned, and I wondered what was happening. I knew that the University of Iowa's Department of Public Safety (UIDPS) officers were unarmed and automatically called in Iowa City Police, who are armed, whenever there was a potential armed encounter. Since I had had no ALG forewarning, I immediately assumed that something in the city had happened and was being followed up on campus. I couldn't wrap my mind around the horrendous nature of the crime I was about to learn about.

My office was situated at the end of a ten-foot long interior passage leading to the open reception area of my suite of offices in Room 114, on the east side and in the middle of the hall, on the first floor of Jessup Hall. I slowly stood up and followed Belinda into the outer office to be met by the serious expressions on the faces of our two secretaries, Cheryl Bates – whom I worked with for more than thirty years – and Sheri Sorge, Mr. Hubbard's former secretary before he retired.

Still in a quizzical frame of mind, I cautiously stepped into the corridor. My instinctive reaction – from growing up on the South Side of Chicago about how to approach "da po-lease" in potentially dangerous situations – was to be sure to keep both of my hands in plain view, follow any commands immediately, and avoid making any sudden moves until my motives were clearly identified by an officer. A police sergeant, that I knew, was coming toward me from the south end of the corridor carrying a pump shotgun. His pistol was holstered.

Before I said a word, in a caring, sensitive, and remorseful tone of voice, he reported, "There's been a shooting in Room 111, and the shooter hasn't been located yet, so please stay and keep your staff in your office with the doors locked because he may still be in the building." With my hands sweating, heart pounding, and body tense, I shakily replied, "Thanks for the information." He said, "The chief will get back to you as soon as we have something to report."

No one from my office reported hearing anything like gunshots. Confused and dazed, I went back into my office to tell my staff the awful news about the most serious threat to the quality of life ever experienced in history at the University of Iowa. My first thought was about my responsibility to console my staff about the possible loss of our colleagues in room 111. Although I didn't have any facts at that point about the shootings, I knew it would be a scary situation for Belinda, Cheryl, and Sheri because our office was where disgruntled students were most often sent with their complaints.

To put the tragedy into context, the press later published the sequence of events:

"...at 3:42PM Initial call to the Iowa City Police reporting shots fired on Jefferson Street, at 3:43PM Report of shots fired in Van Allen Hall Physics Building, (two blocks from Jessup) at 3:49PM Report of shots fired in Jessup Hall."

It must have been about this time that I met the Iowa City Police sergeant in the hall and learned about the shooting in Jessup. Because at 4:01p.m., the gunman was found in a small conference room (203), on the second floor in Jessup with a self-inflicted gunshot wound to his head. He was alive when found. He was handcuffed and died soon after.

At this point, no one in my office knew what had happened. During this serious situation, I couldn't help but be amused by the quizzical expressions on their faces when I went back into the room after my conversation with the police sergeant. Their faces reminded me of little children at Christmas time; the irony was that the surprise was a horror rather than a pleasant surprise.

Cheryl, who generally answered the phones, seemed to be the most anxious and couldn't stand not knowing something about information she had gotten on a call from someone in the building. She said, "I heard that Anne Cleary has been shot." I tried to be cool and convey a calm demeanor, although deep inside I didn't have a clue about how to respond. I said, "I don't know yet, but the police are going to get back to us as soon as they have something to report – so please try to hang on for just a little longer."

Within minutes, although it seemed longer, a police officer pecked on the glass in the window of the office door and beckoned me to come out in the hall. Stiffly, I reached for and turned the knob opening the door, feeling as if I was going to learn something I really didn't want to know. I stepped into the corridor and looked toward the sounds I heard from the south end of the hallway. In the dim light of the hall, I discerned two figures coming toward me, one was the Iowa City chief of police, R.J. Winkelhake, a tall, white-haired, barrel-chested guy, wearing a white shirt with the insignia of his rank on the collar, under a blue waist-length jacket with an ICPD shoulder patch, a black leather duty belt around his waist, holstering an automatic pistol, and carrying a pump shotgun in one hand.

The other person was William "Bill" Fuhrmeister, director of the University of Iowa Department of Public Safety (DPS) wearing a light blue shirt, navy blue waist-length jacket, blue pants, and military style cap with a UIDPS brass insignia, above a shiny leather bill on his cap. Seeing the two of them coming in my direction reminded me of the old style western movies with the cowboy hero wearing a low slung six-shooter, with his unarmed sidekick – because DPS officers weren't armed at that time. In a sense, R.J. had some skin in the game, because his wife, Cathy, was a secretary in the academic affairs (provost) office, although she was in a second-floor office.

I met them about halfway between my office and the south entrance stairwell of Jessup. R.J. spoke in a hushed tone, "We found him," R.J. said with a sad and serious look on his face. "He apparently went into the 203 conference room and shot himself," Bill said. R.J. said, "Two officers found him alive and bleeding profusely from a gunshot wound to his head." They handcuffed him, and he died later. Fuhrmeister said, "He came into Jessup after he shot four people – three professors and a PhD physics graduate student assistant – in a seminar room on the third floor in Van Allen Hall."

Bill continued, "We haven't finished investigating yet, but it appears that he walked from the physics building, where he had shot several people, to this building, went into the academic affairs office, asked the receptionist for Anne Cleary, shot her when she came into the open space at the front of the office, and then shot the receptionist." R.J. added, "We don't know why he went to the room where we found him, but it seems like he may have found the room open, went in, and shot himself. He was dead when the paramedics took him out. Anne Cleary and the receptionist were both seriously wounded and have been taken to University Hospital."

Anne Cleary became my counterpart in academic affairs, after the reorganization of student services departments and programs when Philip Hubbard retired. I was stunned beyond description. But depending on the circumstances, that could have been me. In the years since then, I learned that the news affected me more deeply than I realized at that time. At that moment, however, I felt that I had a job to do – even though I didn't quite know what it was.

I didn't know where to start with respect to the ALG. I asked myself what comes next. This is a major felony murder crime. Do I do anything to coordinate non-police actions? It was about time for offices to close for the weekend; and the weather was getting worst by the minute. Rain was turning to snow with the wind blowing in gusts as darkness descended over the city. Room 111 in Jessup Hall had been secured as a crime scene. University police officers went from office to office informing people that it was safe to leave the building.

The first crisis in communication popped up at this point. Law enforcement officers had secured the building by about 4:30 p.m. Because they were armed, Iowa City police went from room to room searching the building. However, when they gave the all-clear signal, DPS officers went to some of the offices to alert the occupants that they could leave the premises, and they didn't realize that the Office of Affirmative Action, which was directly across the hall from where the gunman was found, hadn't been notified of the all-clear.

The director of the office, Susan Mask – an astute, generally calm, and understanding sepia skin-toned New Yorker, who was quite rational in most situations – was livid when she learned of the all-clear about an hour after the gunman had been taken from the building. She and her staff had been hunkered down under their desks in the dark inside their offices. One could imagine how she and her staff could have been panic stricken hearing the commotion of law enforcement officers and paramedics right outside their office and not knowing anything about what was going on. They were quite relieved once they calmed down from being left in the dark for an extended period.

After the crime scene was secured, most of the people working in Jessup left the building – including Cheryl and Sheri from my office – I then began to feel at loose ends. My heart was racing, I felt numb, and my thoughts were random and unfocused. I was anxious to do something, but I didn't have the motivation to focus on going home. I felt in limbo. I went into my office, turned off the lights, sat in one chair and put my legs across another, leaned back facing the east windows, and stared into the dark gray sky until it appeared to be an abyss. I gradually felt suspended in darkness.

I was stirred back to consciousness by a voice quietly calling my name. Turning toward the sound coming toward me, I looked up to discern the silhouette of Susan Phillips against the backdrop of the dimly lit outer office. "Phil, Phil?" she was calling, "Shouldn't we get the ALG together to respond to the disruption on campus?" Instinctively, I replied, "Yes, you're right." In a call-and-response pattern she responded, "Would you take care of getting that together for us?" I in turn replied, "I'll get on it!"

This wasn't a typical ALG situation. First, law enforcement oversaw the homicide investigations within the jurisdiction of the University of Iowa Department of Public Safety. Most significantly, leaders in the University hierarchy, the president and academic vice president, were both out of town. The usual American university leadership system was out of place.

Our unique set of circumstance that night was out of sync with the hierarchical model of authority, in which authority and power is assumed to be proportional to one's role in the administrative pecking order. In a sense, Susan was the officer of the day under this set of circumstances, and she had had no previous experience in coordinating administrative matters during a campus disruption. In terms of administrative coordination of campus conflicts, I was responsible for functional management of the ALG.

As soon as I heard Susan's voice, I snapped out of my stupor and immediately recognized that she was asking as well as telling me what to do. To deal with the campus disorder and confusion we would need to use the ALG to bring together a collaborative functional coordination group to address the immediate concerns of notifying the families of victims, briefing the press, responding to questions and concerns from students on campus and their families, briefing and receiving input from the collegiate deans, who are the major institutional leaders of the academic colleges of the University, and the Iowa City community at large. I recognize leadership as a group process. I didn't think about feeling bad any longer; I just felt that there was a job to do, and I had to figure out how to get it done.

The events of this tragic situation happened in less than an hour – between 3:42 p.m. and 4:01 p.m. – in the afternoon of November 1, 1991, and widespread chaos struck the campus of the University of Iowa and the Iowa City community. Incomplete reports of mass murder on campus began to appear on local and national radio and television stations minutes after the initial emergency calls were received by the police and paramedics. More importantly, parents had begun calling the president's office, my office, the Department of Public Safety, and the Iowa City police. According to U.S. West Communication, the normal volume of 3,000 to 4,000 phone calls received per hour by the University was exceeded by twice as many calls at about 11,000 calls by 5:15 p.m. from all over the United States and foreign countries.

Susan Phillips and I had virtually no facts about the situation when she brought up the ALG. I learned about the flood of phone calls as soon as I walked back into my outer office. Belinda said, "The phones are ringing off the hook. What do we tell them? We don't have any information yet." This was the first major crisis to address. Dissemination of accurate information is a critically important aspect of crisis management.

The first administrative decision I made was to have all incoming calls to the president's office transferred to the phones in my office. Belinda, with the assistance of June Davis, an administrator in Susan Phillips' office, responded to the incoming phone calls. The most prevalent question was about student residents on campus. The basic response was that students in residence halls and on campus were safe, the shooter was no longer a threat to the community, and further information would be available in periodic releases of information as the police investigation and medical reports became available.

There were several constraining factors, however. Even though we were being made aware of the names of the shooting victims in the Physics Department and in the Office of Academic Affairs, as the calls were coming in, we couldn't immediately release the names until the medical examiner confirmed the conditions of each person, and their families had been informed. Additionally, the shooting locations were crime scenes and had to be investigated by the Iowa State Department of Criminal Investigation from Des Moines – and they were driving from Des Moines in a snowstorm.

The principal role and function of the ALG was getting and communicating accurate, clear, and current information flowing in the immediate hours after the shootings. The composition of the functional coordinating group – that comprised the ALG – varied with the needed expertise for a given situation. We had a core group known as the mini-ALG that consisted of the University's chief information officer, Ann Rhodes, vice president for university relations; the assistant to the president who generally advised on legal matters, Julia Mears, someone from the staff of the vice president for academic affairs, and the director of the Department of Public Safety (or his designee).

After the phones calls were transferred to my office in Room 114 from the president's office in Room 101, Julia Mears, Ann Rhodes, and I sat down in the president's office conference room to begin to figure out what steps to take next, when the phone rang unexpectedly. Julia answered it, listened briefly, and in a pensive tone, said, "Yes, come on over," and hung up. She turned to us and said, "That was Les Sims, he believes he has some information about the shootings."

Leslie "Les" Sims was the relatively newly appointed dean of the Graduate College. A few minutes later, Les – looking very somber – walked through the door. In a slow, methodical, and reluctant way, he rolled back one of the conference table armchairs, sat down, sighed, cleared his throat, and began to speak: "From what I've heard so far, I believe – I hope I'm not right – I think I may know who the person is who did the shootings."

He rubbed his hands together, as all of us leaned forward anxiously. "Before I got here last year, Rudy Schultz (acting graduate dean Rudolph "Rudy" Schultz) was dealing with a complaint from a physics graduate student who was unhappy that he hadn't been given appropriate consideration for a dissertation award from the graduate college. His complaint was against the faculty in the Department of Physics and Astronomy. I believe he also complained to academic affairs. I looked back at the file before I called you and found that his name is Gang Lu, a plasma physics student from mainland China. I don't know if this is actually the case, but it sounded eerily similar when I heard some speculations about the shootings in the physics department."

About that time, the director of public safety, Bill Fuhrmeister, came in the room. We all turned our attention – almost on cue – anticipating clarification of what we had just heard. Bill hastily took a notebook from his inside breast jacket pocket, as he pulled out an armchair to seat himself at the conference table. He began slowly, "Well, the news about T. Anne Cleary isn't good. She was taken to the University of Iowa Hospital and Clinics with a serious head wound, and she didn't make it. She was removed from life support and has died. The student receptionist is in serious condition, and if she lives, she may be paralyzed from the neck down."

"We've identified the shooter," Bill continued. "His name was Gang Lu." There was a deep moan from Les Sims as he whispered, "Oh my God, I felt that he might be the one. It could have been much worst had he gotten to the Graduate College in Gilmore Hall." Though his hands were shaking slightly, in a professional manner, Bill began to read from his notebook the names of the faculty and student killed in Van Allen Hall, "Three professors killed in the conference room were Robert Smith, an associate professor, and professors Christoph Goertz, and Dwight Nicholson, the head of the department, and one of Gang Lu's fellow students, Linhua Shan."

When such a tragedy, as a mass murder happens in an unsuspecting community, it causes a severe sense of personal vulnerability among people in the community. It is completely outside the norm to imagine homicide as part of a learning community. Before learning some of the facts, my sensibilities were paralyzed by my feelings of personal vulnerability.

The unexpected spontaneity of the shootings caused my mind to flash back to a horrendous experience I had in my childhood. One summer afternoon, while playing on a playground, between two parallel, three story public housing buildings, our play was interrupted by piercing screaming and crying coming from the open windows and doors of a third-floor apartment in one of the buildings.

Almost immediately, three black Chicago police cars, a red and white fire truck, and a white ambulance with red stripes, pulled into the short driveway adjacent to the buildings that were elevated five steps above the level of the driveway. The white police officers attracted attention and worrisome comments from people in surrounding buildings, as the residents went from door to door asking their neighbors where the commotion was coming from.

Pretty soon, above the four-foot-high back porch wall on each floor we could see several policemen carefully and quietly ushering people from the building where the screams and crying came from. Several officers stood holding open the screen door to the back door of the apartment. While through the kitchen window, we could see other policemen and paramedics move swiftly back and forth inside the apartment. There was an eerie silence as they frantically went about their work.

By this time, from surrounding buildings, my friends and I were joined on the playground by adults wondering aloud about what was going on in the apartment. Most of the onlookers knew the family living in the apartment. They talked about their friend, the mother and her two small children – a girl about five, and a boy about three. The mother had been living as a single parent until about a year ago, when her husband came home from serving in the U.S. Army during the Korean conflict. The neighbors seemed to have good feelings about the family although some thought the husband was a little standoffish.

It turned out that the mother wasn't in the apartment at that time. She had been taken by the police through the front door of the apartment, down the stairs, out of the building, around the corner, and placed in the back seat of one of the waiting squad cars. People continued to gather, and tension continued to build as everybody wondered why this was happening.

Just as in the case of the spontaneous tragedy on campus, the tragedy in my neighborhood was an unexpected event. Time seemed to stand still immediately after both tragedies, but everything happened within a 15-to-20-minute time frame.

Then two men came out the back door, went down to the waiting ambulance, where they opened the back doors and took out two rolled up stretcher beds. They hurriedly went back into the building, up the stairs, and into the third-floor apartment. Moments later, two figures, each carrying the end of a stretcher bed, emerged from the apartment and carefully came down the stairs. When they came clear of the building we could see a child with heavy bandages around his head covered on the stretcher. Quickly and carefully, they loaded the stretcher into the waiting ambulance. The child's mother entered it before it left with red lights flashing and siren blaring.

A second set of stretcher bearers came out of the apartment, carefully descended the stairs, but not with a sense of urgency came into the clearing, carrying a completely covered body. Among the trailing police and paramedics, there seemed to be a relaxed sense of neighborliness that radiated between the authorities and the residents unlike the tension from the community when the white folks first appeared on the scene.

The reason this childhood experience reoccurred to me in 1991 was that it recalled for me the first sense of personal vulnerability in my lifetime experience that presupposed that spontaneous violence in my community was not expected. Sadly, this is a presumption that no longer exists in many inner-city communities.

The facts of the neighborhood tragedy were that the father, for reasons unknown – but possibly related to a traumatic military experience – went berserk, smashed his son's head with the metal base of a table lamp, and slit both of his wrists with a butcher knife. The screams and crying we heard came from the mother when she discovered what had happened. Despite the emergency treatment given by the paramedics, the father died from loss of blood. The little boy's skull had been crushed, but the paramedics were able to stabilize him, and he survived.

I remember the boy growing up and playing with children in my backyard playground. He had a steel plate inside his skull and a long-jagged scar across his head, a constant reminder of his tragic experience. Why this incident of more than forty years ago came back so vividly to my mind, I don't know, except that it was part of my life experience that gave me some insight about the adrenalin rush that is caused by the fear of personal vulnerability when one feels her/his life is at risk.

Less than two hours after the shooting, we gradually learned the circumstances of this tragedy. The deaths of three physics/astronomy faculty members negatively impacted a renowned international academic and research program. The deaths of two international students from mainland China, one the murderer and the other a victim, negatively impacted the University's largest segment of international students and raised fears of xenophobia on the campus, and in the city, state, and country.

The crisis raised questions about the quality of life for human rights in our community. Once we had specific identification of the victims, the question became when and how their families should be informed of the deaths of their relatives, before the names were released to the media. Away from Jessup Hall, Ann Rhodes created a protocol to periodically brief the media. Reporters were clamoring for details that we didn't have. Subsequent press reporting verified the basic scenario Les related.

The Department of Physics and Astronomy in Van Allen Hall is internationally renowned as the home of astrophysicist and space pioneer, James Van Allen for whom the Van Allen radiation belts around the earth were named. He was also the brother of Professor Maurice Van Allen, MD, whom I had an opportunity to work with in developing the EOP in the College of Medicine, when he was head of the Department of Neurology at the UIHC. One Des Moines Register article observed that the deaths nearly wiped out the department's theoretical space research group.

On Sunday, November 3, 1991, the Register reported witnesses said Lu arrived late at Room 309 for a regular Friday afternoon meeting of faculty and students involved in space theory research. About 10 people were in the room. Students at the meeting said he took a revolver from under his coat. The witnesses said that Lu, without speaking a word, began shooting, firing at Goertz, a professor, and then

Shan, Lu's rival, and then Smith, an associate professor in the department who, before he died, gasped, "somebody killed me."

Lu then scurried down one flight of stairs to Room 208, where Nicholson, the head of the department, habitually left his office door open so that students and faculty members would feel welcome. Another professor in the department, Gerald Payne, said he was chatting with a secretary down the hall from Nicholson's office when he heard one shot. Payne said he ran to Nicholson's office and saw that Nicholson had been shot in the head. "It looked fatal," Payne said. "I could see no sign of life."

Lu then left Van Allen Hall walking west on Jefferson Street about two and a half blocks to the north end of the Pentacrest, where he went into Jessup Hall through the north door on the east side of the building, climbed one flight of stairs to the first floor, turned right, opened the glass paneled door to the Office of Academic Affairs at the north end of the hall, went in, asked the receptionist to see Anne Cleary. The receptionist, a vivacious, social activist undergraduate, was working part-time in her first week on the job. Less than 10 minutes after leaving Van Allen Hall, in Room 111 in Jessup Hall, Lu shot T. Anne Cleary, the associate vice president – my counterpart in that office – and the receptionist, Miya Rodolfo Sioson, when she cried out.

An anonymous letter to the Des Moines Register, dated September 17, described Gang Lu's dispute with the University. In part, the letter read; "Mr. Gang Lu who received his PhD in physics in May 1991, has been filing complaints against Dr. Dwight R. Nicholson, chairman of the department of physics and astronomy, for his fraud in the departmental nomination for the D.C. Spriestersbach dissertation award offered by the graduate college since June, 1991…The graduate college claimed that no wrongdoing was found in this matter."

"Lu then appealed to the Office of Academic Affairs. About a month later, T. Anne Cleary contacted Lu about his complaint. The letter states, "…all Mr. Lu got is 'I will have to call you back.' Days later no word has been heard from Dr. Anne Cleary. Mr. Lu wrote a letter to Dr. Hunter Rawlings III, president of the University of Iowa, on Sept. 13, as his final good faith attempt to have this matter resolved within the University of Iowa."

The final excerpt from the anonymous letter read, "Outraged by the downright(sic) to cover up, Mr. Lu is more determined to pursue a fair resolution to this matter at any cost. And he is considering taking possible legal action if he is left without other choice." It was believed that the letter may have come from Gang Lu himself.

From an investigation, the Johnson County attorney J. Patrick "Pat" White revealed that there had been five letters from Gang Lu detailing his grievances that he gave to friends to mail – four to news organizations and one, written in Chinese, apparently intended to be sent to someone in mainland China. Police intercepted the letters, and Pat White said, "The letters clearly lead me to the conclusion that he premeditated and deliberated his actions."

Unlike any previous campus crisis I had been involved in, this one had no social policy conflicts, free speech controversy, or protesting demonstrators. We had a huge threat to people that created a sense of personal vulnerability. Knowledge of the facts explaining the circumstances of the threat is a significant antidote to relieve feelings of personal danger. Therefore, the major objective of the ALG in the immediate hours after the Gang Lu mass murder-suicide was to communicate accurate, timely, and clear information to the community to allay fears and show empathy for our immediate circumstances.

We needed to convey sensitive and private condolences to the victims' families before public announcements were made in the news media. We had to create a mechanism for students, faculty, and staff to express their grief and compassion for others. And we wanted to find ways to humanize the administrative processes to the extent that, if there were other perceived threats of a similar nature on campus, people would be encouraged to alert the administration to follow up to make a judgment about any potential danger that might be involved.

These challenges didn't fit neatly into a hierarchical power system. Because of the many dimensions of organizational and personal responses required to respond to the emergency, I was sure I didn't have the answers to all the immediate challenges. To create a holistic approach to begin the healing process on the campus and in the community, I felt confident that I understood the process of collaborative leadership and functional coordination needed to bring people together in the immediate hours after the shooting.

Within the first two hours after the shootings – as in other ALG situations – the first things Ann Rhodes, Julia Mears, Bill Fuhrmeister, along with the director of University News Service, Joann Fritz, and Les Sims, and I did was to brainstorm about what each person felt should be done, and how to conduct the first steps to address questions from the media and the public during the immediate three or four hours after we became aware of the tragedy. Ann Rhodes had been in contact with the county coroner who had examined the bodies of the victims in Van Allen Hall and had officially pronounced their deaths.

Our thinking and actions were being improvised at a fast pace. At this point, I made what I considered a serious misjudgment in direction. Two academic administrators who had no experience in the ALG process were in the building while our deliberations were going on, and I incorrectly assumed that it would be more appropriate to ask one of them – because of their stature as tenured faculty members – to be the person to contact the families of the deceased faculty members. One of the professors became quite concerned about why I assumed the authority to direct a professor to do something.

I failed to realize that leadership among faculty, based on academic status and recognition, wasn't necessarily the functional equivalent of the expertise and modicum of power necessary for the gruesome task of informing families of the deaths of their loved ones. Ann Rhodes, however, corrected my misjudgment by calling an associate dean and pathologist in the College of Medicine, Dr. Carol Aschenbrener, who had the professional expertise, personal sensitivity, and humanistic ability to deliver the bad news.

I knew that in an emergency and the time crunch we were working under, that there would be surprises, and, therefore, keeping a flexible frame of mind was an operational necessity.

However, there was a major problem. Although the coroner had conducted the medical examination to pronounce the deaths of the victims, the bodies couldn't be moved until the Iowa Division of Criminal Investigation (DCI) had examined the crime scene. The problem was the weather. The DCI was coming to Iowa City from Des Moines in a snow and ice storm. Within the same hour, we learned that the student, Miya Rodolfo Sioson was going to live but would almost certainly be paralyzed from the neck down. As dean of students – and because no one wanted the job – I was tasked to break the news to her mother by phone in Berkeley, California.

Previously, I had had the unhappy experience of telling a family by phone of the loss of their son. During a biological science summer camp at Lake Okoboji, a student had accidentally drowned, and I had been contacted by the sheriff of that county to contact the parents to have them plan for claiming their son's body. I had to make the call to the parents. I found that there was no easy way to make such a call. You simply must remain calm and sincere as if it were your own family. I called Miya's mother, and she was shocked to the point of speechlessness. She, however, was composed after the initial shock and immediately she began to talk about coming to Iowa City to see about her daughter. She was in Iowa City by Monday morning.

During the brainstorming session, immediately after getting the news from the Department of Public Safety, the group discussed ideas about how and what to inform various campus constituencies about the state of information at that time as well as plans for establishing a safe and peaceful quality of life on campus and in the Iowa City community. Dean Sims mused, "Because individual colleges are not generally involved in campus crisis situations, the nine collegiate deans – who have the most direct leadership responsibility for student learning and faculty activities – frequently voice concerns about being the last to find out what the University administration's position is on resolving campus crisis situations."

Belinda Marner, Ann Huntzinger, and Mary Lynn Grant were a vital link in initiating an emergency meeting with the deans. Ann displayed an innate ability to convey a sense of calm in communicating the critical nature of an emergency meeting as she called each dean to summon to a Jessup Hall conference. Mary Lynn, who created speeches and other communications for the president, radiated a sense of humanism in offering opinions and clarification for communications in written and spoken words during this highly stressful period.

Shortly after we notified the families, the collegiate deans assembled in the president's conference room. As they assembled, there was a quizzical buzz among the deans about what was going on. There was an uneasiness in the air – a feeling like a ship drifting off course – because the hierarchy of the University wasn't in charge of guiding the ship through the storm.

Once they were all in the room, there was a clear sense of confusion about what should be done in the absence of the president. None of us had ever faced a campus crisis the magnitude of a mass murder-suicide. We – like most people on campus – had a feeling of personal vulnerability. They were all talking at once, when something inside me – like the reaction I had when I was at my first administrator/teacher conference in Flint, Michigan, back in 1965 – caused me to speak out in response to the tension in the room: "Everybody, let's calm down, be quiet for a moment, and just relax as we work our way through this." These words came out of my mouth before I realized what I had done. My reaction reflected my orientation in developing social change – as a change agent – to tactfully initiate collaborative leadership.

Nevertheless, as soon as I finished, all eyes were on me. I felt an unexpected, stunning surprise – like a little boy in little league, with the bases loaded, swinging to hit a pitch for a home run – when they all stopped talking and quietly turned their attention toward me. I had succeeded at something meaningful without realizing what it would feel like. After all, these were the most prominent, hierarchical collective leaders in the institution.

I was standing there, feeling naked, when Gerhard "Jerry" Loewenberg, dean of the College of Liberal Arts, spoke up, "I think Phil is right. He has had much experience with difficult situations on campus, and I believe we have a good team of his colleagues to guide us through this crisis in the absence of the president." Jerry's professional status as a leader among the deans legitimized my collaborative leadership position.

What followed Jerry's comments was a relaxed and thoughtful conversation in general agreement that a period of healing needed to begin immediately. They all felt that the ALG was an appropriate way to start a collaborative coordination of a joint campus and community effort to express condolences, show empathy, and encourage spiritual renewal.

As the conversation progressed, it became apparent that there was sympathy for cancelling classes on campus on Monday to begin the healing process. Once the deans felt they were in the loop, they expressed confidence and support for the leadership in the room at that time. A modicum of healing had begun.

Susan Phillips kept President Rawlings informed by telephone. He concurred with the deans' view on cancelling classes. Susan was also concerned about the University's weekend athletic events – since athletics reported to her. A women's varsity volleyball game was scheduled for later that Friday night on campus and there was a nationally televised football game between Iowa and Ohio State scheduled for Saturday afternoon. If classes for Monday were being cancelled, would the University appear insensitive and disrespectful if the athletic events went off as planned? That was a question for the leadership that was influenced by a collaborative decision that had been made through conversations among the collegiate deans.

Women's Athletic Director Christine "Chris" Grant made a compassionate statement to the press about the women's games that weekend: "Considering today's tragic shootings, we think it's only appropriate that we turn our concerns to our friends and colleagues in the University community at this troubled time." In addition, the next day – Saturday – the scheduled match with Northwestern University was postponed pending improved weather conditions.

The Iowa Ohio State game was played as scheduled with a symbolic tribute to the faculty and student victims of the shootings. The Iowa team wore helmets painted completely black – with the yellow center stripe, tiger hawk on each side of the helmet, the American flag, an ANF (America Needs Farmers) decals removed – with only each player's uniform number appearing on each helmet.

While nothing the magnitude of the shootings had ever happened on campus, death caused by murder, accident, and suicide was not unheard of during my tenure, so in the aftermath of this tragedy I thought about how to begin grief counseling in the community as we had done to begin a healing process on the campus. Several years earlier a previous director of the University Counseling Service (UCS), psychologist Ursula Delworth, established a system for responding to psychological emergencies. University counselors worked with the ALG to provide grief counseling for students, particularly those in University housing, but also in other areas across the campus. In this case, however, faculty and staff were also involved.

The UCS director in 1991, Gerald "Jerry" Stone – a down to earth, unflappable, and objectively sensitive licensed psychologist, administrator, and professor – heard the news of the shootings and found a way to contact me by telephone. Within those first frantic three hours after the shootings at about 4:00 p.m., the ALG was working to clarify communications, inform the public, and begin the healing process. Jerry displayed remarkable insight about the depth of grief counseling necessary to address the psychological needs of those faculty, staff, and students affected, directly and indirectly, by the tragedy.

First, he outlined a system for using staff psychologists from the UCS to set up group counseling sessions in residence halls across campus, beginning as soon as Sunday night for those wanting to express their feelings about their grief and personal vulnerability. Next, he thought it necessary to have psychologists on hand in the physics department, beginning on the next Monday morning for faculty, staff, and students in the department, who felt a need to express their feelings about the tragedy. It turned out that it was most beneficial to assign a psychologist to be in residence in the physics department for an extended period.

Obviously, the UCS didn't have student services staff psychologists sufficient to meet the needs of faculty and staff on campus, and there were no University psychologists for faculty and staff services, so Jerry mobilized the professional psychologists in the Iowa City community to work with him – for nominal fees that I arranged for the University to cover – for a brief period to work on campus with various staff and faculty needs.

In addition to a remarkable professional psychologist response, we had a tremendous heartfelt response from the Association of Campus Ministers (ACM). During the 1960s, the link between religious organizations on campus became less formalized in the wake of dismantling in loco parentis. My experiences working with students led me to believe that many of them wanted – and needed – spiritual development and value clarification to create a keener sense of self awareness and confidence. When I became dean of students, I initiated an ongoing dialog, collaboration, and coordination with the ACM for raising contemplative awareness among students who chose to exercise their freedom of choice to participate with the campus ministries.

The ACM contacted me late Friday night to propose an all faith convocation on the following Monday morning in the Main Lounge of the Iowa Memorial Union. They proposed to organize a compassionate program, advertise, make public announcements, and invite a diverse set of speakers from all faiths that wanted to participate. We agreed to their plan and decided to reserve the Main Lounge which was set up for the maximum seating of one thousand. On Monday, November 4, 1991, at 10:00 a.m., more than one thousand people attended the commemoration of the November 1st shootings.

We were aware of the possibility of a xenophobic reaction against Asians because the shooter was Chinese. Asian students were also aware of our nation's historic negative stereotype toward Asians – particularly from "Communist China." Fortunately, Iowa City tends toward being a compassionate and contemplative community, that characterizes the quality of life here. Nevertheless, Asian students kept a low profile in the immediate aftermath of the shootings. They too recognized the reality of dual consciousness in minority status in our society.

While we were trying to figure out how to approach the students without being condescending, I talked to John Rogers, an international student advisor in the Office of International Programs and Services (OIES), during the middle of the first night after the shootings. John told me, "Mainland Chinese graduate students constitute most of the largest segment of foreign students on campus. They are a very self-contained community who support each other. Right now, they are feeling very bad about what has happened. They feel sad about the losses of the lives of faculty, an administrator, and two of their fellow countrymen – one of them the perpetrator – as well as the injuries of a student. They plan to do something to express their sympathy toward the families and the University community."

The students worked with John and his colleagues in OIES to develop a fitting tribute from the Chinese student organization that was presented and read at the convocation.

Once we had endured the immediate aftermath of the shootings on the weekend, there was a heightened sensitivity among some professors and staff about aberrant behaviors they might have encountered – for better or for worst – among foreign graduate students. During the first several days of the following week, I received a call from a professor in the College of Business Administration. I don't recall his name because he spent most of his time recounting a litany of bizarre behaviors by a student complaining about teaching methods to views about professors' competencies.

My antenna for trouble went up immediately. I wanted to know more about the student's background. Was the student male or female, where she/he was from, what was the program of study? The professor unburdened himself of heavy thoughts he had about a potential problem person. He was troubled by the male, master's candidate from India, but wasn't sure what to do besides complaining to his colleagues and college administrators who had also been pestered by the same student.

In checking into the student's background, we learned that he had been enrolled in a graduate program at another university where he had been disruptive and had sent critical and threatening letters to one or more professors. I was curious about this student. After I assembled all the written material I could find about his background, I contacted Jerry Stone at the UCS and asked him to review the materials to get a sense of whether he thought the student had a psychological problem.

After reading the material and talking to the complaining professor, Jerry felt we should proceed cautiously in following up further and before talking to the student. Jerry was concerned that the University not overreact to possible negative stereotypes of foreign students based on the Gang Lu tragedy. After the ALG met to consider the information, we decided to have a conversation with the student.

The conversation was inconclusive, so we decided it might be helpful to talk to someone at his previous university. The follow-up revealed that the student, in effect had been asked to leave the program. By allowing him to withdraw voluntarily and transfer to another university, he could preserve his student visa status, which he might have lost had he been dismissed or expelled. The College of Business didn't know all of this when the student was admitted to Iowa.

Things didn't get any better when we sought to follow up with the student. Jerry expressed thoughts that this could be a person who might "go off the deep end," so we decided to address the question through legal procedures. We decided to have him involuntarily committed for psychiatric treatment.

I learned that committing someone is extremely difficult. The student had to appear before a magistrate for a hearing, which initially seemed to go in the student's favor, until he got upset with the magistrate and tried to reach across the desk to grab the magistrate. The magistrate ruled that the student needed psychiatric help. In the final analysis, the student lost his student status, was referred to US Immigration for deportation, and left the University of Iowa.

In human services organizations, people – not structures – should define the ethos of the institution. However, in response to extreme campus violence, structured organizational methods are necessary to coordinate the complexity of institutional responses for communication, investigation, resolution, healing, follow up, and assessment. I firmly believe that every person with a grievance or complaint should have the right to free expression and due process to address their concerns. But when all administrative appeals have been exhausted, there should be administrative closure.

After the Gang Lu shootings, I initiated an administrative closure process for chronic complaints for which there seemed to be no satisfying a complaining student. Through the ALG we had a semiannual review of – what I called – difficult persons on campus. The process was simple, every person should be given the right to appeal to all administrative offices related to their concern and the various administrators should keep other offices informed of relevant information related to a possible appeal to the next decision maker up the line.

Whenever the appeals were exhausted, the student was informed that she/he could no longer contact an office about their appeal. The process allowed for the ombudsman to be contacted for an appointment, but the complainant couldn't go to the ombudsman without permission from the ombudsman. The only way the complainant could pursue the concern after administrative closure was through legal representation – at their expense. The complainant would be subject to arrest for criminal trespass for violating this procedure.

On November 13, 1991, I got the following letter;

Dear Phil:

I am writing to express my appreciation for your initiative and leadership in forming a team, along with Susan Phillips and others, to manage the crisis of November 1. The University owes a great debt to your clear thinking, steady nerves, and delicate sensitivity to the possible consequences of unfolding events and decisions. Under these extremely difficult circumstances, I could not be prouder of the way the University responded to the emerging situation. I know that much of that response may be attributed to your wise and forethoughtful decisions, and I want you to know that your swift and decisive actions and your careful follow-up work are much appreciated.

Yours sincerely,

Hunter R. Rawlings II
President

Chapter Thirteen:

Environmental Changes

A growing prevalence of abusive drinking challenged the core values of the University and culminated with the death of a student on campus in 1985. Drinking in college is as old as campuses themselves. "Students have always drunk in college" was a constant refrain heard during the development of a crisis of alcohol abuse among students in colleges and universities.

In the 1980s we experienced champagne celebrations at University commencements in the Carver-Hawkeye Arena. By the mid-1990s, it got out of hand. Graduates smuggled bottles of champagne under their robes into commencement exercises. It became so prevalent that some brazenly carried their bottles in full view. There were bursts of sounds of popping champagne corks as awarding of degrees proceeded. Seated graduates drank from bottles of champagne and passed them around with impunity.

After several embarrassing commencements, during an academic deans meeting that I attended regularly, one of the deans wondered out loud, "It seems like graduations have lost their value. Maybe we should consider discontinuing commencements?" Several deans expressed frustration about the behavior of graduates during the ceremony.

At one point in the discussion, someone asked whether there was still any value to having graduations in the arena at all. It was generally agreed that the bad behavior was contributed to by the size of the event. There were a few comments about changing the system of graduation ceremonies – which did happen later, but not at that time. The real question was about how to extinguish behavior that was an anathema to the values of the University.

I weighed in at this point, "I think it's totally appropriate to set reasonable standards for behavior and to have high expectations for students to meet those standards. I think we should create a system to ensure that students learn to respect the standards and communicate the values and expectations for excellence to each other – much as they have done in emulating the bad behavior. We have to stand up for the values we espouse." There was general agreement among the deans, and I got the task to put up or shut up.

Like other social customs, traditional graduation ceremonies were casualties of the social revolution of the 1960s and 1970s. Young people rejected many social mores with distrusting attitudes like "Don't trust anyone over thirty." Because the previous generation had abandoned traditional graduation customs, those coming along in the 1980s had no standards to reject. Therefore, hedonistic behavior reflecting the lowest common denominator became in vogue. Because there was little respect for traditional values associated with the customs and dignity of college graduations, many adopted the attitude that if it feels good, do it – it must be cool.

Changing drinking habits of college students is comparable to creating new social norms in society. The basis of the approach for dealing with champagne toasting during commencements was to reestablish and reinforce traditional collegiate values associated with the end of the formal learning experience with commencement of new developments in – what President Jim Freedman called –the life of the mind.

Use of the public media was considered the most effective tool to create the necessary environmental changes to extinguish abusive drinking. The initial press release was designed to inform, inspire, motivate, and direct graduates to participate in an important event in their own and their parents' lives. Press releases and letters were sent to graduating candidates participating in spring commencement exercises requesting them to cooperate with the "Graduate with Class" campaign through courteous conduct and by dressing appropriately.

They were told that alcoholic beverages wouldn't be allowed, and intoxicated students would be excluded from participation in the ceremony. Appropriate dress was emphasized to subliminally impress upon students, as I was taught growing up, that dressing your best meant acting your best. "We have high expectations that candidates for graduation will cooperate in making this a special occasion for all" was emphasized in press releases and TV interviews.

Little by little, the campaign succeeded. After a few graduations, a new tradition began to emerge void of champagne celebrations during the ceremony. Family members and guests at commencements began to express their appreciation for the sense of dignity and pride displayed by our graduates.

I was responsible for administering policies and guidelines for uses of alcohol on campus for students, faculty, staff, and the public. All University groups were required to get permission from my office for serving alcohol at events on and off campus – and this included recognized fraternities for social events at their chapter houses which are on private property. Undergraduate organizations weren't allowed to serve or consume alcohol at social events on or off campus.

Drinking alcohol is considered by many in our society to be a fundamental right, and no person in authority should have the right to stop them from having a drink. Unfortunately, this belief is held by many college students' parents who believe that drinking in college is a rite of passage. They did it when they were in college, it didn't hurt them, and so it's okay for their kids to have the same experience.

In the fall of 1995 Matthew Garofalo, a young man pledging Lambda Chi Alpha Fraternity, died in the fraternity house because of binge drinking. His death generated a great deal of sympathy for his family. The University was questioned about how it could happen and what the University could do to keep it from happening in the future.

Based on results from a national survey conducted by the Harvard School of Public Health, binge drinking at Iowa was among the highest in the nation at 77%. The University of Iowa is adjacent to downtown Iowa City. Since the 1970s, the campus community developed a reputation as a culture of easy access to alcohol for underage drinkers. In the early '90s, there were more than 50 alcohol licenses within one mile of the campus in downtown Iowa City.

After Garofalo's death, the University participated in a Harvard School of Public Health (HSPH) national study of binge drinking on college campuses. The Harvard college student alcohol (CSAS) study was designed to learn more about the type of drinking college students engage in and the resulting consequences for themselves and those around them. Binge drinking was defined in the study as 5 drinks per person during a two-hour sitting for men and 4 drinks per person during a two-hour sitting for women.

In response to a vigorous public reaction to Garofalo's death and a semester-long moratorium I imposed on alcohol service at fraternity house parties, I initiated a town meeting for anyone to come to voice their concerns, objections, and suggestions as well as for the University administration – the provost, Peter Nathan, the director of student health, Dr. Mary Khowassah, and me – to explain our views, hear public comments and take their suggestions into consideration.

The town meeting was held in the Main Lounge of the IMU. About 150 chairs were set up in the middle of this cavernous space. Chairs for the administration were placed side by side on a three-foot-high raised platform, with microphones in front of each chair on a table in front of the administrators. Dr. Khowassah, Sarah Hansen, director of Health Iowa health education program, and Provost Nathan agreed to moderate the town meeting. I opened the discussion by thanking students and others for taking time out to come and share their opinions.

There was an unexpected participant at the head table. During the fall semester of 1995, Peter Nathan had served as interim University president, while a presidential search was being conducted to select a new president. Mary Sue Coleman from the University of New Mexico had been appointed the new president to take office in January 1996. Mary Sue is a biological scientist, and she was aware of the national issues of student drinking. She became familiar with the Iowa issues on alcohol abuse while interviewing in the fall of 1995. President Coleman participated in the town meeting as her first act as University president.

The audience was a mixture of students, faculty, staff, community members, and business owners as well as a few parents who expressed their view that, "Students in the Greek community shouldn't be considered the same as the unfortunate young man who made a fatal mistake. They should be allowed to continue to monitor themselves in their social activities as they have done in the past."

Changing public perceptions is a critical element of environmental social change. The basic theory of the Advocacy Initiative we implemented with a grant from the Robert Wood Johnson Foundation was to use the media and personal relationships to influence the public and decision makers to focus on alcohol-related problems and solutions. Years earlier when we initiated the campaigns for Safe Saturdays to curtail alcohol drinking in the football stadium, and "Graduate with Class" at University commencements, the media and the public had a cynical and skeptical view of efforts to influence the imbedded social convention of alcohol consumption in society.

This social convention is also connected to the concept of social distance among racial and ethnic groups drinking habits. The Harvard binge drinking survey indicated a national binge drinking rate of forty-nine per cent for white students, sixteen per cent for Black students, and twenty-four per cent for Asians. At the University of Iowa there was great social distance and voluntary segregation where the binge drinking rate was above seventy per cent for white students and Black student binge drinking was about sixteen per cent.

Advocacy initiatives involve new ways of creating social change – as witnessed through the media influence on creating social justice through the Civil Rights Movement. The media ferments development of personal relations and creates allies to lessen social distance in more integrated social settings. In Iowa City, the media kept attention and focus on alcohol-related problems, assessment data, and proposed public policy solutions, while building momentum for legislative changes rather than focusing on problem students.

It's critically important to focus on the effects of binge drinking on the environment from the standpoint of the erosion of the quality of student life in terms of social distance, personal safety, after college professional opportunities, and intellectual and emotional development in a diverse society. It became clear to me that environmental change was about more than the economics of alcohol consumption in terms of creating social change to reduce high-risk drinking. We developed a campus-community coalition – called the Stepping Up Project – to address the educational, social, and economic issues to diminish binge drinking.

The foundation program was called A Matter of Degree (AMOD). Like the tobacco industry, the alcoholic beverage industry exploits young people to create brand loyalty through media advertising that leads drinkers to believe that they are exercising free, hip, and mature recreational social choices. AMOD was designed to use environmental factors to change drinking norms on college campuses.

Apropos to the emphasis on the media, I had an inquiry from an undergraduate African American student named Valerie Holms about creating a class project related to social policy. As we talked about her interests and what might be meaningful for her, I learned that she was a senior from the south side of Chicago interested in social change.

She said:

"I've heard about binge drinking on campus; but I don't know much about it because we don't go to the bars that much – we have most of our parties in the dorms. Is there anything going on to change how people see this situation? Whenever I've been in the bars they seem to play about one Black song an hour. When we get up and dance, the whites stand around and look. We don't buy that many drinks, and it seems like they don't want us in there."

I sensed this might be an opportunity to marry the issue of social distance with high-risk drinking in an analytical way to contribute to advancing quality of life and social integration. Valerie was active in campus life activities as a member of a historically Black service sorority Delta Sigma Theta, and the Black Student Union. I told her how difficult it had been to get favorable press a few years earlier when we initiated attempts to address abusive drinking on campus. She was intrigued by the idea of examining the press to see if media attitudes had changed in the intervening years.

We discussed a project to examine editorials and news articles in the Iowa City Press Citizen (ICPC) the three previous years to assess the editorial bias of the media about high-risk and underage drinking on campus and in Iowa City. In her analysis of the ICPC, she found there had been a gradual shift in emphasis, from a sense of futility about the enforcement of laws and policies against underage and abusive drinking to a less cynical and skeptical view about the sincerity of protestations from some public officials and administrators about addressing the problems.

The shift in reporting bias indicated confidence in the efficacy of the policy proposals, enforcement actions to curtail access and availability, programs for alcohol and health education, and alternative activities being pursued by the campus-community coalition – the Stepping Up Project. The editorial bias showed an expectation of accountability from law enforcement (including campus, county, and Iowa City) and compliance on the part of bar owners and managers in reducing the level of binge drinking in Iowa City. There was a clear endorsement of the positive personal relations being developed among community representatives to create a positive environmental change to reduce high-risk drinking.

Valerie had an interesting response to what she learned from her research. She said, "It was good to learn that binge drinking doesn't really apply to most undergraduate students, including many African Americans." She went on to say, "I realized that we party a lot differently than white students do; Black fraternities and sororities don't party in the bars like the white Greeks do. We mostly party in the activity rooms in the dorms and at the Afro House. Sometimes we have refreshments, and sometimes we don't – and they don't allow alcohol in the dorms and the Afro House."

I interjected, "I don't believe Black students don't drink alcohol sometimes." Her response was: "Mostly the guys get something to drink before they come to the parties. They like to drink malt liquor – Colt '45, like they do in Chicago. I'll be honest with you. We party on Friday and Saturday nights, and since most Black students live in the dorms, they do drink in their rooms before going out – but they be cool about it. Some women mix vodka with fruit punch to drink before they come out. A lot of students do that – not just us."

"Unfortunately, some guys like to smoke dope, but they don't bring it to the parties. The main reason many of us don't go to the bars is because we don't see drinking as the main reason for going out."

To a considerable extent, social distance between Black and white students is defined by the drinking culture. Economics play a big part in industrial drinking at downtown bars. The same is true for tailgating during football season. Black students don't buy beer for huge tailgate parties, but there's no animosity between groups going to games, concerts, or recreational activities on campus.

In the '60s the Motown sound, the Twist, and Cha-Cha-Cha blurred the social distance in popular music and social dance – further narrowed by Hip-Hop in contemporary society – among minority/majority students on campuses. Downtown bars represent an economic social enclave that implicitly perpetuates the historic pattern of segregation in society.

The AMOD summary report stated: "Universities provide ready-made infrastructures for discussion and problem solving and can serve as a base from which to speak out and effect change." University policy changes reflect changes in internal environments and student life. Off-campus environments are more politically and socially complex than campuses. The primary challenge of creating social change in the immediate campus community is establishing and developing a credible long-term commitment from municipal bodies and commercial businesses to address alcohol-related problems. Stepping Up's credibility in the community and on campus increased in relation to the success of coalition proposals and programs in campus areas where Stepping Up had the most direct responsibility.

Creating social change is an everyday proposition. It doesn't happen overnight. After thirty years in higher education administration striving to create change through organizational development, I learned that making progress requires patient, persistent determination on a continuous basis with an understanding that there will be setbacks and successes on the way to evolving democratic, positive outcomes. And there are always countervailing forces, even after initial change has occurred. Between 1996 and 2002-03 binge drinking became a front burner social, political, health, educational, safety, and economic issue on campus and in Iowa City-Coralville. The financing received from the RWJ grant to fund the AMOD campus-community Stepping Up program made the difference.

Through the initiatives of Stepping Up, the Iowa City City Council received several proposals including harsher fines, limiting drink specials, restricting sales to two drinks per person at any one-time, mandatory server training, and eventually a ballot initiative to raise the drinking age to twenty-one. A referendum in 2007 collected 4,258 signatures; 3,333 were needed to secure a place on the ballot for the November 2007 election. The bar owners and managers and a student group called Bloc-21, raised more than sixteen thousand dollars in donations to defeat the ordinance. In the final analysis, there were 8,980 votes against twenty-one only and 6,608 for the ordinance. University of Iowa political sciences professor, Tim Hagel, observed, "Some ballot initiatives take multiple cycles to succeed, and each election more people become educated on the issue which could be the case with twenty-one only."

After the 2007 election there was a sense of resignation among advocates of twenty-one only and in the public. There had been a gradual decline in programmatic activity after the end of AMOD funding but there was still active involvement from Iowa City administration and the Johnson County Department of Public Health, and I continued to fund the position to coordinate a campus-community coalition – which became known as the Committee for Healthy Choices.

I felt anxious about keeping up the momentum to keep people focused on creating social change about high-risk drinking. Most citizens didn't have to confront problems of heavy drinking, loud profane voices, lewd behavior, sexual assaults, fights, and fouled pavement in their neighborhoods. I felt an emotional affinity between furthering equality of educational opportunity and maintaining a safe and healthful educational environment. I was dismayed by what seemed to be an optional choice for something that was a passion in my life.

Fortunately, many of the policies and practices encouraged through Stepping Up initiatives stayed in place, particularly enforcement provisions. In 2010 City Councilor Connie Champion, who introduced and later withdrew support for the 2007 twenty-one-only ordinance, became disenchanted with the attitudes and actions of downtown bar owners/managers. She said, "I warned them if you don't clean up the bars, I will support twenty-one." In 2010 the twenty-one-only ordinance was reintroduced and passed. James "Jim" Clayton, a downtown business owner and coalition member who later became a member of an Iowa state alcohol control board reminded the public, "The ordinance was a major goal of the Stepping Up coalition created by University officials fourteen years ago."

Neither the newly elected mayor in 2007, Matt Hayek, nor the newly appointed University president, Sally Mason, supported the 2007 ordinance for twenty-one-only. However, both favored the twenty-one-only ordinance in 2010. It took a while, but the principles of media advocacy established through AMOD funded Stepping Up between 1997 and 2003 proved to be effective in building community awareness and personal relationships to create environmental social change, even though it took two bites of the apple to reduce access and availability to many underage drinkers in downtown bars.

Chapter Fourteen:

Urbana Invitation

Mary Sue Coleman became president in January 1996. Prior to being appointed vice president in 1997, I functioned as the senior student services administrator reporting to the provost, but sometimes I was "the go-to-guy" in central administration for random problem solving. In the long run my improvisational ability prepared me for the role of vice president and dean of students.

During her first year in office, Mary Sue told me she intended to restore the role of vice president for student services. Prior to my appointment, on more than one occasion, I had been contacted by search firms about vice presidential appointments at other universities. In the fall of 1995, I had a second inquiry to apply for the position of vice chancellor for student affairs at the University of Illinois, Urbana-Champaign. I was familiar with the position, having been invited to apply once before. It's my alma mater. Stanley "Stan" Levy – the retiring vice chancellor – had been a mentor for me in the CIC student affairs/services group for many years. Since we were in a period of transition at the University of Iowa, I decided to explore the possibilities of the position at Illinois.

It was an interesting search process. In addition to the typical application materials such as resume and references, the committee requested current personal news coverage articles if any. I sent a copy of the extensive interview with me by the student writer for a newly created student publication, The Mercury, in 1991. I thought the interview would give the committee an unvarnished look at me from a student point of view. I wasn't looking for a job, so I wanted the committee to have a candid picture of me from the students' perspective. I was characterized in the article as "a potent symbol of UI administration, a negative symbol, a strong administrator, a principled man – or just a cool guy."

I was invited to an off-campus interview with the committee composed of faculty, students, administrators, and staff from the Urbana-Champaign campus. The chair of the committee was a member of the highly regarded College of Engineering faculty.

The interview was conducted in Chicago in a conference suite in the O'Hare Hilton Hotel at O'Hare International Airport, typically used by universities for these sorts of occasions. We sat around a large rectangular mahogany table with a glass overlay on top, surrounded by a dozen black leather Eames chairs with chrome frames and five legs with casters on the ends. Each place setting had a 5x7 inch Hilton Hotel embossed writing tablet in front of it alongside a hotel inscribed ballpoint pen. There were heavy crystal water goblets on the table in front of each setting with two silver water pitchers strategically placed at either end of the table. The room was softly lit by indirect lighting trained on the ceiling and daylight through translucent shades covering expansive windows through which the O'Hare terminal could be seen. I was seated at what was the south end of the table, while committee members arrayed themselves along either side of the table.

These kinds of interchanges are a ritual experience for interviewers and interviewees. Everyone is dressed to impress, while trying to convey a sense of warmth through formality. Committee members are trying to do a hard and thorough assessment of the candidate, while at the same time trying to make a good impression on a valued recruit. While trying not to draw attention to her/his tastes in fashions, the candidate is customarily attired to covey subtle sophistication in a casually elegant way. With comportment to convey interest and understanding of each question and/or comment, the candidate endeavors to respond in clear, concise, sincere – yet not threatening – tones in response to agreeable as well as disagreeable subjects.

I simply tried to relax and be myself. I said what I thought and felt in sincere and candid responses. Apparently, it worked. I was invited to Urbana-Champaign for an on-campus interview. It was quite a different experience than previous trips to the campus. Since Jo's parents lived in Decatur, Illinois – fifty miles west of Champaign – and my mother, who was in declining health, lived with my youngest sister, Carla Dale – a state unemployment claims officer in Champaign – we frequently traveled to the area. Over the years, we occasionally took our children, Phyllis and Joel, to experience the campus.

I had been on campus for professional meetings of the CIC student affairs/ services senior administrators when it was Illinois' turn in the rotation of Big Ten Universities. In March 1988, Stan Levy hired me as an external reviewer of the Office of Student Activities for the Illinois Board of Higher Education review.

When I arrived for my overnight stay at the Illini Union Hotel, I had a calm sensation with anxious anticipation. Calm in comfortable surroundings and simultaneously anxious in anticipation of outcomes of the interviews, I was humbly impressed about being considered for a position at an institution that on my first visit – when I was in high school in 1958 – I was so awed that I couldn't imagine being a student there. It was beyond my imagination that I could ever be considered for a position as a senior administrator in charge of all student affairs/services of the University. It blew my mind!

Despite my initial encounters with racial bias, I have fond memories of being a student at Illinois. My chest swelled with emotion, as I reminisced about the good, bad, and foolish times I had had as an undergraduate. As I walked through the Illini Union onto the tree lined Quadrangle, I remembered the now fully matured trees were newly planted in the early '60s after Dutch elm disease killed the trees lining the Quad in the 1950s. My nostalgia vanished quickly as I began to focus on the administrative, economic, and social structure of this huge multiversity. I began to analyze things I was seeing and speculate about the kinds of questions I might get as I thought about responses I might give in my interviews.

Interviews were conducted in an interior conference room in the Illini Union. In interview sessions ranging from forty-five minutes to an hour and a half, I met groups and individuals from varying colleges, faculty committees, student leaders, student affairs, academic affairs, and central administrators. After two days of about eight hours of interviews each day in the same room, I felt as I did after finishing my PhD degree oral comprehensive exams, tired, relieved, and confident.

I enjoyed the intellectual stimulation, verbal challenges, and direct questions about controversial issues, like, what to do about the controversy of using the Native American tribal name Chief Illiniwek as an athletic symbol. I had no need to hide anything, but also, I realized that sometimes candor can be a weapon that feels threatening to a questioner, especially about social issues reflected from the vernacular side of the veil. So I tried to respond empathetically.

I had dinner with Chancellor Michael Aiken the evening after my second day of interviews. A man of medium stature with an unassuming demeanor, Michael – an internationally recognized sociologist – was provost at the University of Pennsylvania before coming to Illinois. Unlike my interview experience for vice president at Wayne State University in Detroit in the '70s when I dined in the elegant surroundings of the Detroit Club, Chancellor Aiken and I had dinner in a comfortable, modest restaurant in downtown Urbana.

Interviews of this type are more like a getting-acquainted conversation than a question-and-answer session. The chancellor was getting an assessment of my communication skills, thinking ability, and personality from those who interviewed me. He wanted to get a personal feel for my values in relation to his own – just as I wanted to do with him.

We talked about the ongoing protest resulting from the use of the traditional Chief Illiniwek halftime dance with the marching band at football and basketball game halftimes. As a theatrical performance, the Chief is a moving experience; however, midwestern native people protested the inauthentic and perceived disrespectful nature of a white dancer doing a dance in a theatrical costume not representative of the extinct Illini tribe.

I shared with the chancellor my view that, as an alumnus, I appreciated the halftime ceremony, but my views had evolved to appreciate the values native people held for the traditions of their people and I was of the view that the Chief should be phased out. I think the chancellor was of like mind but wanted to proceed cautiously because of the vitriolic backlash among many alumni. Interestingly, I became aware of a similar Native American protest at the University of North Dakota during an accreditation team visit in 2003 which eventually was resolved by phasing out the nickname and mascot symbol "Fighting Sioux."

University central administrative positions are professional appointments without job security beyond quality of performance or preference of the president. A major difference between a non-academic and an academic university administrator is that a non-academic administrator doesn't have faculty rank for tenure in an academic discipline, as does an academic administrator for a fallback position for job security.

I was a non-academic administrator; but never had concerns about not having faculty rank, although I taught and served on masters and PhD comprehensive committees for more than twenty years. I adhere to something my mother constantly emphasized when I was growing up. Take initiative, always do the best job you can, and have integrity in everything you do. Ever since I started in this business, I've relied on these principles as my bases of job security. Creating social change through organizational development was my main goal.

The University of Iowa administration was in transition when I responded to the invitation to apply for the position at Illinois in January of 1996. Samuel "Sam" Becker was the interim provost at the time. I had known Sam since I started the EOP in 1968. As an outstanding scholar and head of communication studies, Sam was committed to equal opportunity and excellence through diversity. He did many things to inspire students and promote social change, such as the time he invited a former Black communications student Greg Morris – an actor starring in the hit television series "Mission Impossible" – back to campus to meet with his students and make a presentation on campus.

I had discussed my invitation to interview at Illinois with Sam days before I went to Champaign-Urbana, so it was no surprise to him when there was a press announcement that I was a candidate for the position. On January 23, 1996, the Iowa

City Press Citizen reported, "Jones was nominated for the job as vice chancellor of student affairs in Illinois first in 1994 and again a few weeks ago. He declined the first time and initially declined after getting a call recently from a search team consultant – hired by the university." In the Daily Iowan, I was quoted, "I am not at all unhappy here at Iowa. I have very deep feelings for the University of Iowa. But if it wasn't for the University of Illinois, I wouldn't be who I am today."

During the first week in February, I was on a Higher Learning Commission accreditation visit to the University of Chicago. Before sunrise, on the morning of the third and final day of the accreditation visit, the phone in my room at the University's guest house rang with a call from the Illinois search firm. The consultant asked me if I was still interested in the vice chancellor position. In a half-asleep and probably incoherent voice, I stammered a response that I was still interested and that I would like to respond more completely after my current assignment in Chicago.

There were a few thoughts prominent in my mind in the pre-dawn morning of February 7, 1996, as I was being asked about my preferences for the vice chancellor for student affairs position at the University of Illinois, Urbana-Champaign. Jo and I had talked frequently about advantages and disadvantages of leaving Iowa. We had never given serious thought to going back to Urbana or anyplace else since I was considered for a similar position at Wayne State University twenty years earlier. She was doing well in her position as business manager at the University of Iowa Museum of Art and was active in civic organizations in town.

Both our children had finished college and graduate degree programs and were out on their own, so our lives were in transition to a different way of being. I didn't have a driving urge to leave Iowa City. I thought it could be a good move, but I didn't feel passionate about it. I was beginning to feel pressure to come to a decision as the flight touched down in Cedar Rapids.

I had left my car at the airport, so I could go directly to my office from the airport. During the thirty-minute drive to campus in Iowa City, I decided on a response to the search firm. I decided that I should seek the best offer I could get, including a possible position for Jo, to consider the move. My financial requirements might be difficult to meet, but I decided that leaving Iowa City would be a significant economic and opportunity loss for both of us.

When I got to my office, I called the search firm with this information a little more than twenty-four hours after I got the initial call on the morning of February 7th. Aside from Jo, I hadn't discussed the offer with anybody else. I never "waved a telegram" for self-ingratiation. Sam Becker and Mary Sue were aware that I was in the pool of candidates for the position at Illinois, but I had not brought it up to either of them.

Toward the end of the day, I received a call back from the search consultant. She said, "The chancellor feels that politically he can't meet your requirements for the position, so he feels he must go in a different direction."

I said, "I think that's fair. I wouldn't want to put him – or me – in an untenable position in the institution." To which she responded, "Would you consider withdrawing your name from consideration?" Since this is what I expected, I said, "Sure, I don't have any difficulty with that."

I drafted a brief statement to fax to Chancellor Aiken. But before I sent it, I e-mailed a copy to Sam Becker. A few minutes later, there was a rap on the half-closed door to my office. I looked up to see the trademark bowtie and youthful looking crew cut of Provost Sam Becker coming through the door. With a relieved expression on his face, he sat down in the chair next to my desk, sighed, and said in a near whisper, "Thank you for your note. I'm sure there are a lot of people here who are glad you've decided to stay."

I honestly didn't think many people would have that sentiment. I guess that's what comes from assuming how others feel on the majority culture side of the veil.

By early Thursday afternoon – a little more than 48 hours after being contacted in Chicago – I sent my withdrawal statement to Chancellor Aiken. Technically, I was never officially offered the position by the University of Illinois, Urbana-Champaign. All my negotiations had been through the search firm.

On February 12, in an email, Chancellor Aiken wrote:

Dear Phillip:

Now that the dust has settled, I am writing to let you know how very much I enjoyed meeting and speaking with you during our search for a Vice Chancellor for Student Affairs. I felt we had a common understanding of the appropriate place of Student Affairs in the life of a university, and I was extremely impressed with your thoughtful and energetic approach to the many issues we discussed. My colleagues who met with you were similarly impressed. You should know that your visit left you with a great many admirers on this campus.

Thank you very much for your willingness to consider this position. I am proud to be able to call you an alumnus of this university and I am confident our paths will cross again very soon. I look forward to that.

Chapter Fifteen:

People Not Structures

There were no immediate changes in my position or in the Division of Student Services immediately after I withdrew from the search at Illinois. I was comfortable with my situation. In a way, it was a risky state of mind. I was elated that I was accepted in Champaign, exactly opposite of my emotional state when I first arrived in Champaign as a student thirty years earlier.

To maintain psychic equilibrium, I learned a long time ago to take the bitter with the sweet and people at face value. I, like many Black people, have come to a point characterized by psychiatrist Alvin F. Poussaint as sophisticated skepticism. It's an American narrative as old as the constitution and is something we live with on both sides of the veil.

I believe in the University of Iowa. My responses to two opportunities to leave for vice presidential positions at two different universities demonstrate my allegiance to this University. It has the heart and soul for social change built into its DNA – although it should be prodded occasionally. At this critical point in my career, I felt sanguine that Mary Sue Coleman and Sam Becker embodied the same view of the University I had been oriented to, so I didn't worry about what they would do about reorganizing student services. I would accept whatever outcome there was – and if it didn't go my way, so be it. I would survive and go on to something to continue to create social change and equality of opportunity in education.

Throughout her first year, President Coleman observed, studied, analyzed, and assessed central administration, its officers, and the University. She talked to me on several occasions about the organizational rational for student services and its strengths and opportunities for improvements. Near the end of her first year – eight or nine months after my interviews at Illinois – she began to talk to me about what she planned to do to reorganize the Division of Student Services.

In her assessment of me, she said she'd gotten favorable and critical views of me – she heard I could be inflexible sometimes. I responded, "I've always maintained that if an idea makes sense, I'll support it, even if I don't like it. But if an idea doesn't make sense, I'm not inclined to be supportive, even if it's something I personally like. I'm as consistent in decision making as the information I have at the time. I am inflexible about unfair treatment of people or disregarding the right to due process or ignoring the disadvantaged."

Near the end of the year, President Coleman completed her assessment of central administration. She decided to reestablish the vice presidency for student services and promoted me to the position. She said, "The change is a step toward meeting the University's strategic goal of fostering a high quality academic environment, while providing additional advocacy for students and contributing to a greater focus on student life issues."

University of Iowa Student Government (UISG) president Marc Beltrame expressed similar sentiments, he said, "I think this is an exciting development because it gives student life a stronger position at this University… Most research schools in the country have this arrangement." Marc indicated that President Coleman had discussed the new position with him well before the move was made. The Daily Iowan reported that Beltrame said, "This change has come about because of President Coleman's commitment to a high-quality student life. As vice president, Jones will now be part of the president's cabinet and should be better positioned to serve the interests of the student body."

The philosophical basis for my administration of Student Services was on my concept of functional coordination. The rationale for my approach is based on the organizational complexity of the University and the multidimensional aspects of student life. To implement functional coordination student development concepts, student services staff and administrators assume multiple roles that may have short-term, intermediate, or long-range implications in vertically structured reporting organizations and/or horizontally formed functional groups.

Horizontal organizations are often temporary task-oriented teams designed to achieve a specific objective, and membership in the horizontal organization, or functional group, is based on expertise relevant to the task or purpose for the person or group. Because of the interrelated nature of student life activities, functional coordination involves departments, programs, offices, and colleges outside of the Division of Student Services.

Consistent with the ethos that people, not structures, make a great university, President Coleman reassigned to me Dean Hubbard's previous responsibilities as dean of academic affairs for Old Capitol and the Natural History Museums because she felt I could coordinate their efforts. I was asked to coordinate direction with University of Iowa Hospitals and Clinics (UIHC) for Student Health Services. I coordinated reporting to her for the University of Iowa Alumni Association, the Robert Wood Johnson Foundation grant for the Stepping Up Project, and I became the University administration non-voting representative to the executive committee of the Iowa City Chamber of Commerce – responsibilities not typically associated with student services.

My orientation to university administration was based on my beginning experiences as an EOP director. I was brought in as a change agent to navigate between activist Black students and status quo white administrators. I had to create credibility with the students and the bureaucracy. I learned to work across the institution and develop allies for unconventional approaches to address students' needs.

As I advanced through administrative responsibilities, I realized that the same basic principles I learned as EOP director were relevant and applicable to university administration, peer review for federal education programs, classroom teaching on cultural diversity, consultant-evaluator of universities and colleges, and membership on national panels for policy development. Through the support, encouragement, critical appraisal, and expectation of excellence from the presidents, vice presidents, faculty colleagues, and other administrators I developed multiple improvisational approaches to create social change through organizational development.

Increasing diversity of a student body requires a broad range of educational and personal support programs outside the norm of traditional student services. As EOP directors, we learned that the hard way when Black students in the '60s protested for social, cultural, and intellectual inclusion in the life stream of the institutions. Women, Latino, Native American, Asian-Pacific Islander, gay, lesbian, bisexual, and transgender, and different ability students followed suit.

Undergraduate international students were vigorously recruited in the 2000 decade. They brought increased revenue through higher tuition and a need for new depth of cultural awareness, respect, and sensitivity to their need for personal and educational support programs outside the norms of traditional U.S. historically underrepresented groups on campuses. Student diversity requires – and demands – a broader range of competencies and range of behavioral services, cultural programs, language, spiritual, and academic support to address the needs and desires of a more ethnically, racially, and internationally diverse student body.

The needs of students with wide ranging learning abilities and behavioral development needs must be recognized and addressed. Through contemporary student recruiting media markets and personal contacts, parents maintain constant contact with their students and demand equity for those from diverse backgrounds.

Socio-cultural problems of the broader society also affect the university environment through the behavioral practices of students from many different backgrounds. Drugs and alcohol abuse, physical and sexual assaults, thefts, and vandalism affect university communities in rural and urban settings. Functional coordination of support services, housing programs, counseling services, law enforcement agencies, and university disciplinary procedures are central forces for equitable, non-discriminatory constitutional due process, and prompt disposal of cases of criminal behavior or disciplinary misconduct.

My primary focus was building the infrastructure of student services. The president charged me with producing a sound, progressive, financially defensible, need based proposal that incorporated students' input to present to the Iowa Board of Regents for funding through student fees. Having had experiences as a consultant-evaluator assessing CIC and other peer universities, it was clear to me that for Iowa to remain a viable choice for recruiting undergraduates in the 2000s and beyond, we needed to create a set of sound alternatives to enhance the student services infrastructure.

I knew that if I wanted to transform the student services infrastructure, I had to devise a comprehensive plan based on documented needs for change and updating facilities and services. I had begun to develop wellness centers in residence halls and there was a limited fitness facility in the Halsey Gym across from the IMU. The campus Field House – where most of my classes for my master's degree in physical education took place – was both an athletic and recreation facility. There was a clear need for a comprehensive campus recreation wellness center dedicated primarily to student use – and athletics secondarily.

The philosophical basis of my master plan to rebuild the student services infrastructure was a report from the Carnegie Foundation describing the campus as a purposeful learning community. In a planning meeting with student services directors, Gerald "Jerry" Stone, the deep thinking, sensitive, and plain-talking director of the University Counseling Center said, "We need an arrangement for student services like the various pavilions in the University hospitals. We need a student services pavilion." That became my vision for a student services master plan.

Student services departments were located at various locations on the east and west sides of the Iowa River. Developing a cogent master plan for such a widespread, eclectic organization proved to be a daunting task. I wrote a proposal to present to Richard "Dick" Gibson, founding director of the Department of Facilities Services. I had known Dick ever since I came to the University, when he oversaw the space assignment office for the University. He was responsible for the multiple office moves and renovations I experienced in changing positions over the years. Dick had a sharp eye for critical detail. Proposals had to be clear, concise, and to the point. We had several conversations before I could convey the essence of my omnibus proposal in clear and convincing terms.

Dick recommended bringing in Ken Bussard as a planner – the architect whose former firm, Bussard Dikis, planned and designed the 1988 renovation of the Iowa Memorial Union. After receiving a clear picture of what we wanted to accomplish in developing a master plan, Ken recommended using Brailsford and Dunlavey, a relatively young facility planning firm formed in 1993 and run by a sharp, articulate African American, Paul Brailsford, and a talented architect, Chris Dunlavey.

We developed a process based on conversations with students, faculty, and staff to learn their impressions of the campus as a purposeful learning community. Delivery of student services was dictated by where they were located on campus. During the previous four decades, little investment had been made in space specifically designed and dedicated to students. Research indicated that the University of Iowa ranked last among peer institutions in wellness/recreation space per student. Understanding the relationship of services to student needs determined the affinity of services by proximity.

The master plan was my template for future planning and/or improvisation. The plan was for a town square linking a student services super center to living/learning neighborhoods on the west, east, and north campuses.

Consistent with President Coleman's directive to produce a sound, progressive, financially defensible, need based proposal, after a series of conversations with campus constituents and a survey of six thousand randomly chosen students, we produced a report that indicated a high demand for a renovated student union.

My strategic approach for developing the master plan was based on a series of four questions. What am I up to? What do I want to accomplish? What does it cost? What are we willing to pay? Listening to and surveying students and others began the process to address the first three questions. What are we willing to pay was the most critical question for student responses. Most students supported extensive renovations at a sixty dollar per semester fee.

Unlike the 1960s, when students protested from outside the university making demands for social change, minority administrators like me were now on the inside. I had learned that creating meaningful social change requires more than platitudes. We set out to create a clear, plain, understandable word picture that the president, vice presidents, and members of the Iowa Board of Regents would agree to support. I considered the results from what we heard in purposeful planning to be the functional equivalent of the list of demands from earlier days of the movement for social change, or a translation of images from my vernacular or improvisational experiences into descriptive facts I acquired through learned or documented experiences.

Initially, the planning process centered on the IMU, but during the listening phase, we learned that there were strong desires among students for a comprehensive east campus recreation/wellness facility. Consequently, we made a study, like the IMU study, for a comprehensive east campus recreation/wellness facility. Most students, faculty, and staff had favorable responses to a proposal to develop a new improved recreation and wellness facility.

Ken Bussard, Paul Brailsford, and Dick Gibson recognized the need to develop tangible options for creating an east side campus recreation/wellness facility. Based on impressions from my initial vision, they created a process to describe word pictures of designs, with accompanying costs to create a tangible visualization of each option. Survey respondents favored a comprehensive wellness/recreation facility on the east campus and renovations to the Field House.

Proposed designs for the IMU first, second, and third floor plans were designed to relocate some offices and services and to create spaces for potentially new opportunities to be included in the renovated student center. An exciting new three-story atrium/pavilion was designed to be constructed on the patio on the east face of the IMU. Additional opportunity space was created for moving the offices of the vice president for student services by eliminating three meeting rooms on the southeast corner of the IMU's second floor.

At the end of our planning process, I felt diminishing psychological tension, lighter physical pressure, and more self-confidence about the functional coordination process. I felt admiration for the team of administrators, consultants, faculty, students, and staff who worked through the democratic process. I was convinced we had created a product we could proudly present to the president, university financial planners, and Board of Regents.

For many years, the Board of Regents had designated a portion of tuition for specific purposes such as student activities, student services, and debt services for buildings. We produced a thoroughly convincing and defensible plan. President Coleman believed it should go forward in a different format than the traditional budget requests for student services funding requests. Mary Sue and Douglas "Doug" True, vice president for finance, a very savvy financial planner, decided to make a proposal to separate mandatory student fees, for student services, from tuition allocations.

"In October 1999, the Board made a fundamental change in the structure of tuition and fees at the University of Iowa to establish new mandatory fees for certain student activities and student services rather than using tuition revenues." (From

Board of Regents minutes, September 2001).

About the same time as we were completing the student services purposeful plan, the Department of Athletics was in the process of planning renovations for the football stadium which required removal of the Klotz outdoor tennis courts – named for the legendary Iowa tennis coach – outside the south end of Kinnick Stadium. They proposed moving campus recreation facilities to the west campus adjacent to the completed Roy G. Karro Athletics Hall of Fame – at the corner of Melrose Avenue and Mormon Trek Road, west of the Finkbine Golf Course. According to the Board of Regents summary, the plan contemplated construction of a 150,000-gross square foot Athletic/Recreation Building with a natatorium for instructional and competitive swimming and diving, 6 indoor and 12 outdoor tennis courts.

The Board of Regents deferred the athletics project, due to the schematic design and limited availability of funds provided through athletics. The Board expressed concerns about the proposed facility in relation to student services planning. In addition, the Board addressed the need to consider the University's comprehensive plan for the development of campus recreation facilities before it could reconsider the Athletic Department's project. The Board cited the study done for student services planning by Brailsford/Dunlavey indicating a severe shortage of space per student, particularly on the east campus.

Prior to this point in history, recreation program planning had always been secondary in the development and use of athletic/recreation facilities on campus. For the first time, the purposeful planning process gave primacy to students in the development of recreation/wellness facilities for the University.

The Regents document indicated that the project would be funded through revenue bonds supported by an increase in student building fees and user fees paid by non-students. From our surveys, we had hard evidence that students had repeatedly provided a strong message that they wanted to change the pay-for-play system that had previously supported recreation programs at a minimum level of operation. They were willing to support an increased student fee to secure modern recreation/wellness facilities dedicated to the student body.

The Board minutes stated: "The Master Plan for Student Services (1999) provides a

framework for future planning to meet student needs at the University of Iowa which had a shortage of recreation space per student, particularly on the east campus."

My thesis from the beginning of this initiative was that developing new spaces to enhance the quality of student life would advance social change. I would be less than candid if I said I had no recurring doubts and anxiety about how to translate my existential vernacular impressions into terms of the learned tradition and documentation of bureaucratic reasoning. I was elated to read the Board of Regents documents that reflected the outcomes we sought to create through the purposeful planning process. In September 2004, the Board gave the University permission to proceed with the East Campus Recreation /Wellness Center and the Field House renovation project and phase one of the new Iowa Memorial Union construction and renovation project.

Although Mary Sue Coleman was no longer at Iowa – she became president of the University of Michigan in 2003 – her leadership set the tone for a significant escalation in the quality and expansion of the University of Iowa student services infrastructure. With her leadership, we sought to show that, in developing new space, emphasis should be on expanding opportunity and creating an environment that motivates all students to seize new opportunities in a diverse learning environment.

Right after she got mandatory student fees segregated from tuition, she asked me what I thought about moving my offices to the IMU. I said, "We've thought about it before. There could be some real and symbolic reasons for doing it, but we couldn't do it before without taking away from student resources. I didn't want to create offices for student services in space secondary to what we have in Jessup Hall." At which point, she interrupted me, "Oh no, the offices will be first rate!" Mary Sue talked the talk, and she walked the walk. She meant what she said, and she delivered.

In 2001, the Office of the Vice President for Student Services was relocated to the second floor of the IMU on the southeast corner of the building, to three former meeting rooms, two of which had been offices for conference programs, and a third, on the southeast corner of the floor, was the Grant Wood meeting room. The president made funds available for what became a unique set of internal glass-walled offices with an entry designed to reflect the glass paneled entries of the administrative offices on the first floor of Jessup Hall.

The IMU is an actual and symbolic metaphor for social change in the second half of the 20th century and in the new millennium. As the student center, it mirrored the social mores of a segregated society during its early history. It was also the launching pad for social dissent during the Civil Rights Movement and the war in Viet Nam. Indeed, the Iowa Memorial Union is named in recognition of men and women who served in the armed forces during the two world wars, Korean conflict, the war in Viet Nam, and wars in the Middle East. The Iowa Black alumni recognized the significance of the IMU as a metaphor for human rights when they chose to have the Black Hall of Honor portraits hung in the IMU.

President Hunter Rawlings wanted to recognize the legacy of Philip G. Hubbard after he retired in 1990. The park space on the south side of the IMU which is used for a myriad of gatherings, events, classes, and informal relaxation had been renamed Hubbard Park in recognition of this remarkable person. Construction of the IMU addition presented an opportunity for a broader recognition of Mr. Hubbard's legacy. On a wall inside the east entrance of the addition is a bronze plaque of Mr. Hubbard which describes him as a research engineer, Dean of Academic Affairs, Vice President for Student Services – the first Black vice president in the Big Ten – and the first African American tenured professor in the history of the University of Iowa. The statement cites his dedication to the agenda of public education and his gentle perseverance toward the goals of inclusion, acceptance, and fairness during his years of service to students. Mr. Hubbard's ethos is engraved in the stone wall of the building east entrance: "The antitoxin for intolerance is human kindness…respect for the dignity of each person and a concern for the welfare of human kind."

In 2003, President David Skorton – who knew, worked with, and admired Philip Hubbard during David's twenty-year history as a member of the College of Medicine's faculty before becoming a vice president and then president of the University of Iowa – proposed to the Board of Regents to name the new building addition the Philip G. Hubbard Pavilion and Commons along with the expansive first floor lounge in the new addition, the Hubbard Commons.

State legislation requires new University constructed buildings to designate up to one-tenth of one percent to purchase or create works of art in public places. A six- foot-tall, bronze sculptured statue of a dramatic female figure by Elizabeth Catlett was selected to be installed in the Hubbard Commons. A metal plaque posted next to the statue reads: "Catlett, one of the most celebrated American artists, chronicles deeply political stories and experiences of African Americans and Mexicans, especially women." In 1940, she became the first student to complete the Master of Fine Arts Degree at the University (where the degree was created). Grant Wood urged her to work on subjects she knew best, for Catlett this meant African American women. Hence, the universal figure, Stepping Out.

An art gallery in Hubbard Commons is named in honor of Jean Kendall, former director of the IMU. Jean, a long-time staff member of the union in many capacities, gave aesthetic direction to the IMU. She was involved in establishing a high school art project in the lobby of the union, created a program to install original art by Iowa artists in each room of the Iowa House Hotel, and graphic art displays of Iowa culture throughout the corridors of the Iowa Memorial Union.

University of Iowa Campus Recreation & Wellness Center

IOWA MEMORIAL UNION

Transformation of the Student Services began with the addition and naming the Philip G. Hubbard Pavilion and Common. (https://vp.studentlife.uiowa.edu/awards/hubbard-human-rights-award/)

Stepping Out by Elizabeth Catlett

Chapter Sixteen:

The Sweatshop Movement

I n April 2002, the University experienced its first major campus disruption since the Anti-Apartheid Movement in the 1980s. Students Against Sweatshops (SAS) organized to protest poor working conditions, workers' rights, and fair wages for people in foreign countries making wearing apparel sold by colleges and universities. Students opposed university affiliations with an industry-controlled association, the Fair Labor Association (FLA), that monitored trade practices of foreign contractors. In its place, students nationwide supported a coalition named the Workers' Rights Consortium (WRC) as an independent monitoring organization to investigate labor conditions in factories around the world producing collegiate apparel.

The University's affiliation with the FLA was through the product licensing program of the Department of Athletics that had an exclusive licensing arrangement with companies such as Nike and other companies. After listening to the positions of SAS and explanations from the athletic department for supporting monitoring efforts of FLA industry initiatives, President Coleman said to me, "We need to find out what other Big Ten universities are doing and how they're going about responding to these demands on their campuses."

I started by calling my counterparts on Big Ten campuses. Institutional reactions and responses to the FLA/WRC controversy were all over the lot – responsibilities were fragmented to athletics, legal departments, purchasing departments and assistants of campus presidents and chancellors. President Coleman organized a conference call among relevant campus administrators. I alerted the student affairs/ services administrators whether they were directly involved or not. On the first conference call, Mary Sue coordinated the flow of information. It was stunning to listen to her lead a strategic conversation in a casual, comfortable, and cordial way – about a topic that many were uninformed or uncomfortable talking about. She moderated the first two conversations before we got all the appropriately involved people to continue conversations in the future.

The sweatshop movement on campus began with a campaign to raise awareness of and financial support for the WRC. It wasn't a widely known set of issues among student organizations at Iowa. Most students didn't appreciate the significance of a connection between deplorable labor conditions in sweatshops in Central America and Asia and tee-shirts, sweatshirts, and other college logo apparel they wore every day.

The WRC cause was hampered and made obscure by the fact that many clothing companies in America weren't subject to the WRC mandates. From the standpoint of the American worker, sweatshop conditions were directly connected to outsourcing of American jobs to cheap labor sources in underdeveloped countries. Workers' rights demands were made against universities that got large financial returns through exclusive licensing agreements with manufacturers that produced and sold wearing apparel bearing university logos and trademarks. The complex nature of the business arrangements among Big Ten universities was the subject of the initial conference calls.

Unlike the anti-apartheid divestment movement against South Africa, there was no clear target of social justice. The reason organized labor joined the SAS protest was the basic issue, namely, losing jobs in this country to cheap labor in emerging markets. Exploitation of people in poverty situations is as old as human history, after all slaves built the pyramids. Women and children are easy targets for less demanding, low skilled jobs of clothing manufacturing.

Modern forms of forced labor involve unsanitary and unsafe working conditions, long hours with no relief, and semi-imprisoned work environments – in other words, slavery by another name. The FLA was an industry initiative to blunt criticism of exploiting people for high company profits that redounded to the benefit of universities. Many observers, particularly from non-governmental organizations (NGOs), reported gross violations of human rights. The WRC was formed to counter an apparent conflict of the industry backed FLA.

As an independent labor rights organization, the WRC had no dedicated funding base. Therefore, students decided that relevant universities had a financial interest and a moral obligation to support a credible monitoring organization to ensure fair labor practices. Boycotting the industry wasn't a viable option for organizers because a boycott would simply kill the jobs of the people being exploited. Since such companies as Nike, Reebok, and Adidas had exclusive contracts to provide shoes, shirts, uniforms, helmets, balls, and other athletic equipment for universities, the most productive strategy was to demand that universities support WRC to monitor sweatshops producing many of the products provided to universities by the contracted companies.

We had done our homework to understand the issues in the protest movement. A critical lesson I learned from President Boyd and his administration was that, whenever there is a potential social protest, the University should establish a principled position consistent with the fundamental role of the University as a forum for the free exchange of ideas while at the same time respectful of human rights issues involved in the protest.

It's not an easy thing to do; but it's far better to stand for something before there are protests and campus disruptions, than to have to respond to the forces of protests to simply restore functions on the campus. Proof of this point, for me, was in the outcomes of protests I experienced over the years against recruiting on campus by the CIA, anti-apartheid demonstrations, and controversial speakers on campus. I learned that the best way to promote social justice is to articulate human rights positions that may not be what either side agrees to but that allows for free expression, while at the same time, minimizes disruption of the University.

President Coleman didn't take a position for or against students against either organization. But rather she took a position that would best work most effectively – given the information available at the time to all we had consulted with – to increase monitoring of working conditions in faraway places as well as in exploitative situations closer to home. After weeks of study, consultation, and conversations, she announced that the University of Iowa position would be to contribute to both the WRC and the FLA. I agreed. I felt that to make the greatest impact, it made the most sense to be part of both organizational efforts. It wasn't a position for or against either organization but rather an attempt to exert the most effective political pressure to achieve the desired outcome for social justice.

Students against sweatshops didn't agree. They weren't satisfied with any recognition of the FLA as a monitoring organization of labor exploitation in sweatshops around the world. Our position, however, gave the students a hook, or rationale, to create a cause by claiming that the University supported despicable labor practices for the benefit of corporations and university athletic teams at the expense of unknowing students who flock to purchase licensed university athletic wear.

Student militancy on the sweatshop issue evolved from verbal advocacy to direct action during 2001-2002. There were many opportunities for them to make their case to the president and to the press during Mary Sue's monthly open forums for student interests. The sweatshop movement never became a major priority for student government leaders or the Daily Iowan.

In March 2002, there were rumblings about direct actions to protest University involvement with the FLA. At the same time, I was invited to be a member of a Higher Learning Commission accreditation team to review higher education in the United Arab Emirates for possible recognition by U.S. higher education institutions. The trip was scheduled in the month of May 2002.

I felt conflicted about going to the Middle East versus staying on campus as student militancy increased. Emotionally I really wanted to go to the

UAE, but logically I felt I needed to tell the president that if she wanted me to stay on campus I was prepared to do that. When I told Mary Sue how I felt, her face and eyes brightened, as she spoke with a prideful voice, "Oh no Phillip, that's such a great opportunity, I wouldn't want you to miss it."

To attract student attention, Students Against Sweatshops set up several tents and about a half dozen chairs on the lawn of the Pentacrest south of the Jefferson Street and Cleary walkway intersection, between Jessup Hall and MacBride Hall. They intended to conduct teach-ins during the day about sweatshop issues, recruit supporters to the cause, and to stay overnight on the lawn until the University changed its position to support their demands. Although camping on the Pentacrest was in violation of University policy, with the organizers' cooperation, we worked out an agreement to accommodate their purpose. We convinced them to agree that there would be no sleeping in the tents overnight. Ostensibly, people would stay in shifts to continue dialog throughout the night with students who were out late – coming home late from the bars or other nighthawks.

Soon after the encampment began, President Coleman held a strategy meeting away from central campus, across the river, at the Levitt Center for University Advancement. She invited the vice presidents, general counsel, faculty senate officials, public safety director, a university relations person, a past central administrative official observer, and me. While she had no students at the meeting, she and I had been talking to protest organizers and student government leaders for weeks.

Harkening back to my experiences at the end of the anti-apartheid demonstrations, I made an impassioned plea to uphold the principled position President Coleman articulated and to support both the FLA and the WRC even in the face of protests by outside groups like the United Steel Workers from Des Moines.

I remembered how sad I felt after the apartheid protests, speaking with tears forming and a lump in my throat as I described to President Freedman and the administrative group how we had to arrest more than one hundred protesters because of the long delay by the administrative group in deciding about the University's position. With passionate emphasis, I expressed how important I felt it was not to delay making decisions to end the sit-ins when it was clear that the right to assemble became disruptive or unsafe. We had an honest and serious discussion about the efficacy of the University administration taking any position in what might be perceived as a labor organization and management conflict.

I have a vivid memory of my clear sense of responsibility, when at the end of the meeting – as we were filing out of the third-floor meeting room – the president quietly and calmly took my elbow, held me aside while others left the room. She spoke in a low, calm, serious voice, "Phillip, I think you need to be here if we have demonstrations." There was a consensus in the meeting that the sit-ins – unlike the teach-in encampment that the students ended on their own – would likely have to be ended by the University, if not by the protesters. I respected her reassessment of a potential campus disruption and without hesitation, I accepted her decision – which sounded more like a gentle request than an administrative direction which was her prerogative.

I called the Higher Learning Commission in Chicago to tell them I couldn't make the trip to the United Arab Emirates. I was asked, "Do you know someone at Iowa, who knows that part of the world, who might take your place?" I was dumbstruck. I couldn't imagine how I could possibly find someone on such short notice – especially since I believed I wasn't personally acquainted with anybody with such characteristics.

It occurred to me that I might look to the Office of International Programs or the Graduate College to learn if there were any faculty members who might be familiar with the Arab World, who could make the trip on such short notice. I was committed to try, but I really didn't think there was any chance that I would be successful.

Without much faith in the possibility and feeling a little stupid, I called the graduate college office for research. I said to the person who answered the phone, "I have a strange question and request that I'd like to know if you can help me with. I was supposed to be part of an accreditation team for the Higher Learning Commission to go to the United Arab Emirates next month to review several institutions of higher learning, and at this point I can't make the trip. Do you think there is anyone on campus with knowledge of higher learning institutions in that region, a valid passport, and appropriate immunizations that could stand in for me on such short notice?"

She listened patiently and didn't laugh at me. Then spoke confidently, "Let me think about it, talk to my colleagues here to see if we can come up with a response, and then I'll call you back." To my astonishment, she called back in less than a full day. "There is a faculty member who knows that region well and has visited there recently," was her opening comment. The fact that Axel Ruprecht, a professor in the College of Dentistry, had lived in Saudi Arabia, worked with an academic partnership program to admit students in dentistry from the Kingdom of Jordan, and had recently traveled to the region, was pure serendipity. I talked to Axel to thank him for going in my place. It turned out that his going worked well for the HLC and the University of Iowa – especially the College of Dentistry.

I recalled the saying, "the more things change, the more they stay the same." Reminiscent of the anti-apartheid movement, I dreaded the prospect of removing protesters if their actions became disruptive to the functioning of the University. Students camped in the corridor of the first floor of Jessup Hall for four days and nights. The University safety engineer assessed health and safety conditions of the corridor at the end of four days and determined that their occupation had led to unhealthy and unsafe living conditions for themselves and others occupying offices and classrooms in the building.

Consequently, protesters were directed to end their occupation and to voluntarily leave the first-floor corridor of Jessup Hall. Unlike the anti-apartheid demonstration, a few left voluntarily, about twenty-five were removed, cited, and released by the University's Public Safety office (no outside law enforcement was necessary), and only four were arrested at their insistence.

I was proud to have been part of the process to address the sweatshop issue on campus. I have great respect for and learned a lot from Mary Sue and the way she analyzed and acted on what, in some people's minds, was a capitulation to the opposition to the protesters. She was given great praise, however, by many others including members of the Board of Regents and by major financial supporters of the University.

For my part I value greatly a handwritten note I received in the mail at home from Mary Sue that more than made up for missing the trip to the United Arab Emirates.

She wrote;

"Dear Phil, you were simply superb this past week! Thank you so very much for your leadership and support. You make me very proud to be associated with the University. I really am sorry that you had to give up the trip to the United Arab Emirates, but I hope you know my trust in you was paramount in my decision to ask you to stay"

Many Thanks,

Mary Sue.

Epilogue:

Privileges and Responsibilities

Intrinsic rhythm and momentum for organizational social change in an institution is proportionate to the social values of the institutional leadership. I always felt I had support from the University leadership whenever I initiated a program or planned to advance social change. Much has changed and much still needs to be accomplished to achieve true equality of educational opportunity for educationally and economically disadvantaged students in higher education.

Organizational development to achieve equality of opportunity has evolved through societal responsibility to increase racial, ethnic, religious, sexual, and contextual diversity. Personal responsibility for social justice has resulted from changing social norms for broader advocacy for inclusion, personal development, and free expression. Creation of special programs was an extension of the Civil Rights Movement in the 1960s, accompanied by mass movements, legislative changes, and economic realities as precursors of broadened responsibility and social privilege in society and in higher education.

I don't accept the notion of a post-racial America since the election of the first African American president of the United States. However, there is no question that America has a more welcoming attitude toward so-called racial and cultural differences, which must be related to the expansion of educational opportunities in higher education. I benefited personally and professionally from increased opportunities to assume ever-increasing responsibility and garnering of social privilege through my education and professional experiences.

I descend directly from a depression era, urban migration generation. My life began at zero. My mother had no husband, no home, and no money – and I had no name. She worked to earn responsibility and social privilege and taught her children to strive always to be worthwhile, take initiative, and strive for a better life than the one we started with. I learned that assuming responsibility to get things done is a privilege of living in a free society. I am a product of my environment, where I learned that "freedom ain't free" and that there is still a lot to do to create a more perfect union.

Social change is shown in population polls demonstrating a liberalization of social norms during the past five decades. The election of Barack Obama is the most dramatic evidence of broadening social norms since the assassinations of John F. Kennedy, Robert Kennedy, Martin Luther King Jr., and Malcolm X in the 1960s. Derisive racial and ethnic slurs that were once acceptable within social speech is no longer tolerated in social discourse.

Normative expectations have changed to the point that many people with reactionary viewpoints have created and use coded symbolic language designed to veil derisive comments and actions to promote subliminal negative stereotypic images of socially unacceptable views. Unfortunately, explicit and implicit bigotry still exists. Fortunately, however, broader social norms lead many people with social privilege to take responsibility to reject the veiled, subliminal, negative racial and cultural stereotypes couched in learned traditional language with the symbolic inference to deprive people of human rights.

In the 1960s, when I was in my twenties, I thought civil rights legislation would remove legal discriminatory barriers, but I didn't believe it would change biased attitudes. In concert with the reality of double consciousness, I decided to work for social change, consciously aware of but not worried about racially biased attitudes. Those perceptions colored my thinking as I began my work at the University of Iowa. Through the years I experienced an evolution of feeling and thinking related to a liberalizing of social norms in society.

I was inspired by the support and recognition I received in assuming responsibility at the University for developing equality of opportunity components across the University. From the vernacular side of the veil I – like many of my Black colleagues across the country – had a cynical view of negative attitudes we encountered in responding to the national crisis that Black students protested on campuses across the country. The University of Iowa has been a great laboratory for social change in the extension of the Civil Rights Movement.

I came to appreciate that African Americans weren't the only people negatively affected by historic discriminatory mores in society. There are white folks who feel the sting of discriminatory social norms – even though they may not have been directly discriminated against. Many of them initiated and carried out changes in the institutions that were beyond the reach of entry level EOP bureaucrats. People with the mindsets of Sandy Boyd, Philip Hubbard, Jim Freedman, Hunter Rawlings, Mary Sue Coleman, and David Skorton were the instruments of changing social norms that are reflected in contemporary social policies that have moved from tolerance to acceptance, to appreciation of racial, cultural, physical and learning disabilities, and sexual orientations in this institution and in our society.

President Sally Mason inherited an institution with a history of higher expectations for advancing human rights. She seemed to demonstrate a laissez-faire attitude toward social issues. She showed little appreciation for community concerns about abusive use of alcohol on campus and in the community among students. She sought to use an informal resolution to avoid negative publicity to resolve a complaint of sexual assault. When confronted by an investigation by the Iowa Board of Regents, she used subliminal cues of negative racial stereotypes to blame me. Her actions abused the privilege of her responsibility by shifting blame to protect her presidency.

Nevertheless, I've experienced how the majority community of Iowa City, and nationwide in a general sense, as the embodiment and transmission of values of the learned tradition in society, have expressed rejection of coded subliminal discriminatory cues, in various forms of bigotry, perpetuated by reactionary forces to limit the social privileges of the historically underserved and ignored in society. Most people know the subliminal cues for negative racial stereotypes. Interpretations are not limited to those with double consciousness.

In the final analysis, I'm proud of the people I worked with – in and out of the University – and contributions we made toward advancing social change and human rights in the University as an extension of the Civil Rights Movement in society.

NOTES

Bowen Convocation

EQUALITY AMONG MEN
an address By Howard R. Bowen, President, The University of Iowa

April 9, 1968 to honor the memory of Dr. Martin Luther King Jr.

Martin Luther King was a forward-looking man. He presented to America-not recrimination for past injustices nor hatred growing out of past indignity. Rather he presented a vision for the future to be accomplished by awakening the conscience of the American people. He said, "I have a dream that one day this nation will rise up and live out the true meaning of its creed: We hold these truths to be self-evident, that all men are created equal."

It is up to us today, in the spirit of Martin Luther King, to look into our own consciences and ask: what can we do - we who are students and staff members of this University and citizens of Iowa City-what can we do to help Dr. King's dream come true.

We cannot by ourselves solve the national problem of equality among men, but with a great University at our disposal, we can help.

At a time of national sorrow and shame, it is easy to give vent to our emotions through rhetoric, and then when the shock subsides to fall back into an all-too-familiar routine. The test of our conscience comes not from what we say, but from what we do. And it comes not from what we do over one weekend, but rather what we do in a sustained fashion over months and years.

In the past few days, I have discussed with students and staff the question of what we should do. From these discussions have emerged six concrete proposals. I shall present them to you and ask for your support for them.

First and foremost, I should like to ask a new sense of dedication and commitment on the part of every member of the University, every citizen of Iowa City, and every organization to the cause of equality among men. No one of us – white or black – has a clear conscience in this matter.

Second, I suggest that individually and in groups we consider the current state of federal and state legislation regarding civil-rights, education, economic opportunity, and express our views to Congressional leaders. It is obvious that bolder and more comprehensive provision for jobs, family income, education of the disadvantaged, and housing are needed without delay.

Third, I ask that the steering committee of our new and successful Actions Studies Program explore opportunities for relevant study and community service. We need to enlarge our understanding of the Afro- American culture, of interracial relations, of poverty, human rights, and related matters.

Fourth, the Dean of Faculty, Mr. (Willard) Boyd, is making plans to convene a meeting of interested faculty members to review our educational and research activities in the area of Afro-American culture, interracial relations, poverty, etc., and to consider the introduction of new courses or programs. This group will include faculty members from areas such as Law, Medicine, Dentistry, Nursing, Education, the School of Letters, Economics, History, Political Science, Sociology, Religion, and Social Work. This group will undoubtedly consider the establishment of an interdisciplinary center or institute of Afro-American studies, and will also probably consider linkages to the recently established and exciting program on human rights.

Fifth, the University has been involved for several years in Upward Bound, which is financed mainly by federal funds, and also in assistance to LeMoyne College and Rust College, both are predominantly Negro institutions located in the Memphis area.

I ask that we continue and strengthen these programs. I particularly hope that we shall carry on and extend our increasingly active relationships with LeMoyne and Rust College. These institutions, though, are doing more for Negro education than we shall ever do, and they deserve our continuing support. They have expectations of help from us which we should not disappoint. The fact that they are located in the Memphis area, where Dr. King died, perhaps gives them special significance. I would suggest that the local committee - RILEEH as it is known – be strengthened by the addition of faculty, students, and citizens of Iowa City. Sixth, I ask that we join together – students , staff, and Iowa Citians – to welcome more students of Negro and other minority backgrounds to study at the University of Iowa. The University has been working on this objective for several years and we know it is not easy to achieve. There are problems in locating qualified students, there are problems relating to the nature of our community which in spite of good intentions is not always hospitable to minority groups, there is need in some cases for special programs and tutoring, and most of all the cost for financial aid is very heavy. But these are difficulties to be overcome, not reasons for inactions. I expect to authorize the Dean of Admissions and Records to increase his staff for the express purpose of identifying and counseling qualified Negro and other minority students and helping to open the door of opportunity for them at this University. But when these students arrive, they need substantial financial aid, and the University funds in this area are very limited. Here is where we can all help. I suggest that we establish the Martin Luther King scholarship fund, and that we – students, faculty, townspeople, and friends of the University – contribute to this fund. I am thinking of a fund of perhaps $50,000 a year. This in combination with modest loans would provide opportunities for perhaps 35 to 50 additional students of minority background. These students would be known as Martin Luther King scholars. Their scholarships would perpetuate on this campus the name and the ideals of the man we honor today. Would you be willing to support such a program? The cost might be shared more or less equally among students ,faculty, and townspeople. The cost to students would be of the order of a dollar or two a year. I have invited a small group of students, faculty, and Iowa Citians to serve as a steering committee to consider the establishment of the Martin Luther King Scholarship Fund. They will report in a few days, and if they recommend the creation of the fund, then plans for raising the money will go forward promptly. Your help will be needed both in solicitation and in giving.

Don't feel you must wait for the official campaign. Send your contributions to my office today, and I will see that they are used for scholarships for Negro students. Also please let me know by post card or telephone how you feel about the Martin Luther King Scholarship Fund.

I have presented a six-point program by which those of us here in Iowa City might begin to do our part in carrying on the ideals and the work of Martin Luther King. The program doubtless could be improved. It strikes me as perhaps too small and too unimaginative in relation to the dream of Martin Luther King. If you have ideas that are better, please come forward with them. In the meantime, let us get to work; let us make a new beginning.

CIC NOTES

The Committee on Institutional Cooperation (CIC) is currently named the Big Ten Academic Alliance. Chief academic officers from each university are the official institutional representatives to the CIC. A discussion about establishing educational programs for the educationally disadvantaged was a central topic at the CIC annual conference in the fall of 1967.
Excerpts from CIC minutes of the March 20-21, 1967 meeting documented the initiatives and efforts the CIC made to begin addressing educational and social inequality in higher education. The CIC chairman conveyed the request of a University of Illinois group for an inter-institutional conference on the disadvantaged student. The chairman explained that this concerns those young people who deserve to enter college but, because of a number of all-to-familiar social and economic problems, do not have the opportunity to do so.

On April 24, 1968, the CIC voted to establish a Subcommittee on the Disadvantaged to consider problems arising in this area of concern on the member campuses. Members agreed that a meeting of faculty and staff representatives from member universities should be arranged to consider such matters as recruitment and retention, remedial programs, counseling, financial aid, curricular programs (such as African American Studies), student activism, personnel and employment policies. The CIC chairman appointed Willard L. "Sandy" Boyd from the University of Iowa to chair the subcommittee.

As a result of the CIC subcommittee meeting in Iowa City, plans were made to hire staff at each university and to initiate programs for the disadvantaged. The next annual CIC meeting was held in Oakbrook, Illinois, in the fall of 1968. Present at that meeting were black administrators who had been hired to represent this initiative at CIC institutions (which also included the University of Chicago in 1968).

We were there for the first time to begin what became institutionalized policy and practice to create social change in higher education that has led to subsequent goals to achieve excellence through diversity in colleges and universities across the country.

Toward the end of the Oakbrook meeting, Clarence Shelley, the newly appointed director of the "Project 500" at University of Illinois, Urbana-Champaign raised his hand to be recognized. He rose ceremoniously and asked, "What is the purpose of a Black Dean?" The room became eerily still. The chief academic officers had not anticipated the reaction of the newly appointed black administrators. As the tension subsided in the room, the moderator said, "I think you should have a meeting to discuss that question." I raised my hand to volunteer to organize a meeting in Chicago before the end of December.

The CIC conference of directors and coordinators of special programs for the disadvantaged was held in Chicago, Illinois, at the Bismarck Hotel in December, 1968. Thirteen CIC universities were represented. The list of conferees and their titles were indicative of the concentration of appointments in student affairs which was the most flexible administrative area to concentrate a new emphasis in institutional missions to address issues of equity for the educationally disadvantaged students.

The summary of the two-day conference indicated that conferees discussed the spectrum of day-to-day problems involved in assisting economically and educationally disadvantaged students on member campuses. Recommendations included more emphasis on recruiting more non-disadvantaged black students, more real authority for directors to respond to student needs for community involvement, and a more tangible commitment and involvement of the total university in expanding equal educational opportunities, not just specific departments and central administration. They also stressed that program administrators should be more fully oriented to university policies and procedures.

The conferees were:

Larry Hawkins, Director of Special Programs, University of Chicago
Clarence Shelley, Director, Special Educational Opportunity Program, University of Illinois, Urbana-Champaign

James Briggs, Director, Educational Assistance Program, University of Illinois, Chicago

Rozelle Boyd, Assistant Dean, Junior Division, Indiana University, Bloomington

Phillip E. Jones, Coordinator, Educational Opportunity Program, University of Iowa, Iowa City

John Chavis, Coordinator of Special Programs, University of Michigan, Ann Arbor

Lloyd M. Cofer, Vice President for Special Projects, Michigan State University, East Lansing

Eugene R. Briggs, program consultant, University Student Union, University of Minnesota

Paul H. Black, Assistant Dean of Students, Northwestern University, Evanston, Illinois

William E. Conley, Special Assistant to the Vice President for Student Affairs, Ohio State University, Columbus

Frank Hale, Ohio State University, Columbus

Ann Redman, Office of Special Counseling Services, Purdue University, Lafayette, Indiana

James Baugh, assistant director of special program University of Wisconsin, Madison

Merritt Norvell coordinator of minority graduate student recruitment at the University of Wisconsin, Madison
Samuel D. Proctor, Dean of Special Projects, University of Wisconsin, Madison

Ernest Spaights, Special Assistant to the Chancellor for Educational Opportunity, University of Wisconsin, Milwaukee

University of Iowa academic administrators and faculty played significant leadership roles in the CIC to expand educational opportunities for historically under-represented racial groups in Big Ten Universities and peer universities nationally. Alvin Scaff, Associate Dean of the Graduate College at the University of Iowa, chaired a CIC subcommittee that prepared a formal proposal for foundation support of a project to enlarge the pool of black doctoral students at CIC universities. These initiatives were precursors to the Summer Research Institute Program (SRIP) held on alternating CIC campuses to develop minority potential for doctoral study.

A survey of Afro-American studies in the CIC with respect to their structures, teaching personnel, and accreditation was initiated and conducted by University of Iowa Professor of English and American Studies, Robert "Bob" Corrigan who led pioneering efforts to establish Afro-American Studies as an academic discipline at Iowa and in the nation. Bob became the long-time distinguished president of San Francisco State University.

" While one should not judge a book by its cover, the title does capture the essence of this book. Phillip Jones presents values and messages of his early upbringing and education as an African American and how he carried these messages as an administrator at the University of Iowa. His story is not just one of dealing with bureaucracy and attending structures, but of shaping structures and attitudes so that they became more responsive to new generations of students, especially students of color.

When Phil left the University of Iowa in 2008 it was a more inclusive, sensitive and honest place than it had been in the the over 40 years since he started. Phil shares his insights, observations, and experiences regarding some of the most significant events that helped shape the University of Iowa during his tenure. This is a highly readable and inspiring biography by a man who saw opportunities not obstacles, who saw colleagues not competitors, and who met "failures" with atry

Nicholas Colangelo, Ph.D.
Dean and Director Emeritus
College of Education
University of Iowa

" Phil Jones has written a fascinating and informative professional biography about how a senior black administrator negotiates increasing bureaucracy and race at a major American research university. It is highly recommended reading for anyone interested in understanding how American universities work and conduct their business."
--Dr. Ernest Pascarella
    The Mary Louise Petersen Professor of Higher Education at
    -The University of Iowa.